Research & Education Association

The Best Teachers' Test Preparation for the

GACE®

Professional Pedagogy

Patrick A. Hannigan, Ed.D.

Armstrong Atlantic State University

Savannah, GA

Visit our Educator Support Center at:
www.REA.com/teacher

Research & Education Association
61 Ethel Road West
Piscataway, New Jersey 08854
E-mail: info@rea.com

The Best Teachers' Test Preparation for the
Georgia GACE® Professional Pedagogy Test

Printed in the United States of America

Library of Congress Control Number 2008942503

ISBN-13: 978-0-7386-0414-5
ISBN-10: 0-7386-0414-3

The competencies presented in this book were created and implemented by the Georgia Professional Standards Commission and Pearson Education, Inc., or its affiliate(s).

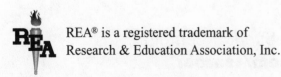

REA® is a registered trademark of
Research & Education Association, Inc.

About Research & Education Association

Founded in 1959, Research & Education Association is dedicated to publishing the finest and most effective educational materials—including software, study guides, and test preps—for students in middle school, high school, college, graduate school, and beyond.

REA's Test Preparation series includes books and software for all academic levels in almost all disciplines. Research & Education Association publishes test preps for students who have not yet entered high school, as well as for high school students preparing to enter college. Students from countries around the world seeking to attend college in the United States will find the assistance they need in REA's publications. For college students seeking advanced degrees, REA publishes test preps for many major graduate school admission examinations in a wide variety of disciplines, including engineering, law, and medicine. Students at every level, in every field, with every ambition can find what they are looking for among REA's publications.

REA's practice tests are always based upon the most recently administered exams and include every type of question that you can expect on the actual exams.

REA's publications and educational materials are highly regarded and continually receive an unprecedented amount of praise from professionals, instructors, librarians, parents, and students. Our authors are as diverse as the fields represented in the books we publish. They are well-known in their respective disciplines and serve on the faculties of prestigious high schools, colleges, and universities throughout the United States and Canada.

Today, REA's wide-ranging catalog is a leading resource for teachers, students, and professionals.

We invite you to visit us at *www.rea.com* to find out how REA is making the world smarter.

Acknowledgments

We would like to thank Larry Kling, Vice President, Editorial, for his editorial direction; Pam Weston, Vice President, Publishing, for setting the quality standards for production integrity and managing the publication to completion; Alice Leonard, Senior Editor, for project management and preflight editorial review; Diane Goldschmidt, Senior Editor, for post-production quality assurance; Christine Saul, Senior Graphic Artist, for cover design; and Rachel DiMatteo, Graphic Artist, for test design.

We also gratefully acknowledge Carolyn Duffy and Mary O'Briant for copyediting, Aquent Publishing Services for typesetting, Ellen Gong for proofreading, and Brooke Graves for indexing the manuscript.

About the Author

Dr. Patrick Hannigan's career spans forty-three years. He began as a public school classroom teacher, serving for twelve years; he then spent twenty-five years as principal of two Blue Ribbon schools, culminating this portion of his career as a central office administrator for three years. He is now an assistant professor at Armstrong Atlantic State University, Savannah, Georgia, in middle and secondary education. Dr. Hannigan had previously spent nearly twenty years as adjunct faculty at the University of Rhode Island, Rhode Island College, Salve Regina University, and Johnson & Wales University—all in the field of teacher preparation.

Contributors

Fred Storar, social studies teacher at Arthur Williams Middle School in Jesup, Georgia, holds a bachelor's degree in business management from the University of Maryland, University College. Currently, Mr. Storar is enrolled in graduate school at Armstrong Atlantic State University in Savannah, Georgia, pursuing a Master of Arts in Teaching, in middle grades education.

Jamie Burchett Danford, a graduate of Armstrong Atlantic State University, is currently completing her Master's in Teaching at AASU. A native of Savannah, Georgia, Jamie plans to teach language arts at the secondary level.

Pamela Mahan, DSN, MA, RN, an assistant professor of nursing at Armstrong Atlantic State University in Savannah, Georgia, teaches health promotion, theory, health policy, and community health nursing. Mahan received a doctoral degree from the University of Alabama at Birmingham. From 1993 to 1996, she was a National Institute of Occupational Safety and Health (NIOSH) educational grant recipient, with a research focus in work-environment stress and stress management with secondary school teachers. She is also a former high school biology teacher.

Susan Croom, a graduate assistant in middle and secondary education at Armstrong Atlantic State University, served as editorial assistant to the primary author.

Contents

Introduction

About This Book

REA's *The Best Teachers' Test Preparation for the GACE Professional Pedagogy Assessment (Test Codes 171 and 172)* is a comprehensive guide designed to assist you in preparing to take the GACE Professional Pedagogy Assessment. This test was created to assess the knowledge and skills of individuals seeking an alternative route to teacher certification.

To teach in the Georgia public schools system, prospective educators who have not completed a state-approved teacher preparation program are required to pass the GACE Professional Pedagogy Assessment (Test Codes 171 and 172) as well as the GACE Basic Skills Assessment and the appropriate GACE content area assessment. This is the *testing approach* to certification, as opposed to the traditional approach, which requires you to take courses through a college system, a Regional Educational Service Agency (RESA), or a university.

To help you succeed in this important step toward your teaching career in Georgia schools, this test guide features the following:

- An accurate and complete overview of the GACE Professional Pedagogy Assessment
- A targeted review of each subarea

- Tips and strategies for successfully passing the test

- Diagnostic tools to identify areas of strength and weakness

- Two full-length, true-to-format practice tests for each part of the Pedagogy assessment based on the most recently administered GACE Professional Pedagogy Assessment

- Detailed explanations of each answer on the practice tests

When creating this test preparation guide, we at REA considered the most recent test administrations and professional standards. We also researched information from the Georgia Department of Education, professional journals, textbooks, and educators. The result is the best GACE test preparation materials based on the latest information available.

About Test Selection

A teacher may be certified by the state of Georgia in several ways:

The traditional route. This route to certification has three possible pathways. The first is the one taken by an undergraduate who completes a bachelor's degree program in education, meets all Georgia state requirements, passes the GACE content area assessment if appropriate, and is recommended by the college or university for a certificate. The second pathway applies to post-baccalaureate students in education who complete their certification requirements after having received an undergraduate degree in an area other than education. Last, educators with an existing certificate from out of state can have their certification transferred to Georgia through reciprocity. In all these cases, the initial programs are completed prior to being employed as a teacher and result in a clear, renewable certificate. Those taking the traditional route are not required to take the Professional Pedagogy Assessment.

The alternative route. This path, also called the testing option, is for career switchers who already hold degrees in areas other than education. It is these prospective educators for whom the Professional Pedagogy assessment is specifically designed and expressly required; they must pass this GACE assessment—along with the Basic Skills and content area tests—in order to earn their certification. Those pursuing this alternative route often enhance their knowledge of teaching, and thus their preparation for certification, through RESA programs, internships, or coursework at a university or college.

Your decision to utilize the alternative route, or testing option, to certification should not be taken lightly. The GACE tests are designed to measure your proficiency in the basic skills of reading, writing, and math, and to address the specific content area that you will be teaching. You may be in a highly technical career field, or perhaps you are quite experienced in a particular discipline. However, the GACE content area assessment will examine your currency in the discipline, particularly as it applies to Georgia Performance Standards (GPS). Be aware that those who are poorly prepared for the GACE tests may find the content questions and even the basic skills questions difficult. Be assured that this Professional Pedagogy study guide is designed to ease the way for you, but the elements in it need to be used systematically.

The GACE assessments are offered during morning and afternoon test sessions, each of which is four hours in length. The number of tests you may register to take in one test session is determined by the assessment(s) for which you are registering. Each assessment consists of one or more tests. The Professional Pedagogy assessment, for example, consists of two tests: Test I (Test Code 171) and Test II (Test Code 172). Because you are registering for an assessment that includes multiple tests, you may opt to take both Professional Pedagogy tests in the same test session. The tests are not individually timed; you may take as long as you need on each test, but you must complete both tests within the four-hour time period.

Note that Tests I and II of the Professional Pedagogy assessment are administered *only in the afternoon* of all test dates. The afternoon session has a reporting time of 1:00 P.M. and ends at approximately 5:45 P.M. (Always check the GACE website for any changes in test dates or times: *http://www.gace.nesinc.com/*.)

Remember: The Professional Pedagogy assessment is only for those who are seeking certification using the testing option (alternative route).

About the GACE Professional Pedagogy Assessment

The Professional Pedagogy tests (171 and 172) contains 60 selected-response (multiple-choice) questions each and constructed-response (essay) questions. You are allowed to use up to one full page for each of the essay questions.

What Do the Tests Cover?

The following table lists the objectives used as the basis for the GACE Professional Pedagogy, along with the approximate number of questions for each subarea in the tests. This book provides a thorough review of all the specific skills covered by the tests.

Professional Pedagogy Assessment Framework

Test I (Test Code 171)				
Subarea	Objective	Skill	Approximate Number of Selected-Response Questions	Approximate Number of Constructed-Response Questions
Student Development and Learning	0001	Understand human development, factors that affect development, and how to apply this understanding to promote student learning	30	1
	0002	Understand learning processes, factors that affect student learning, and how to apply this knowledge to promote student development and learning		
	0003	Understand student diversity, how to apply this knowledge to promote learning for *all* students, and how to foster appreciation and respect for diversity within and beyond the classroom		
Learning Environment	0004	Understand how to establish a safe, inclusive, and positive learning environment that fosters learning, equity, and excellence	30	1
	0005	Understand strategies for creating an organized and productive learning environment, and for promoting students' ability to monitor their own behavior		
	0006	Understand principles and practices of motivation and communication in the classroom, and how to apply this knowledge to promote student learning and encourage active engagement in the learning process		
Total Number of Questions			60	2
Percentage of Score			80%	20%

			Approximate Number of Selected-Response Questions	Approximate Number of Constructed-Response Questions
Subareas	**Objective**	**Skill**		
Instruction and Assessment	0007	Understand types of assessment; the relationships among goals, assessment, instruction, and learning; and how to apply various assessment strategies to support standards based instruction	30	1
	0008	Understand curricula and instructional planning procedures, and how to apply effective planning to design instruction that promotes learning achievement for all students		
	0009	Understand various instructional approaches and principles of instruction, and how to apply this knowledge to provide students with effective and appropriate learning experiences		
Professional Roles and Responsibilities	0010	Understand how to promote positive, productive relationships among school, home, and community to support and enhance student learning and well-being	30	1
	0011	Understand how to work effectively with colleagues; reflect productively on one's own teaching practice: seek feedback from a variety of sources; and update and strengthen one's professional knowledge, skills, and effectiveness		
	0012	Understand the rights and responsibilities of students, parents/guardians, teachers, and other school personnel in various educational contexts, and the legal and ethical guidelines for educators in Georgia		
Total Number of Questions			**60**	**2**
Percentage of Score			**80%**	**20%**

Table title: Test II (Test Code 172)

How Are the GACE Tests Scored?

Your total raw score is converted to a scaled score. A scaled score is a combination of the number of scorable questions you answer correctly on the selected-response section of the test and the scores you receive on any constructed-response assignments. They are then converted to a scale from 100 to 300. The score of 220 is the passing score for any GACE test. The passing score for each test is established by the Georgia Professional Standards Commission and is based on the professional judgments and recommendations of Georgia educators. "Pass" or "Did Not Pass" status is based on your total score for each test. If you meet the passing score, your total test scaled score is not reported in order to preclude the use of GACE scores for purposes other than Georgia educator certification (e.g., employment, college admission screening).

Test I and Test II of the GACE Professional Pedagogy assessment are scored separately, and the passing scaled score for each is 220. There is no composite or combining the two tests. You must pass each test.

When Will I Receive My Score Report?

Your score report will be mailed to you on the score report date listed on the "Test Dates" page of the GACE website (*www.gace.nesinc.com/GA3_testdates.asp*). Your scores are reported directly to the Georgia Professional Standards Commission and are automatically added to your certification application file. Your scores are also reported to the Georgia institution of higher education or other agencies that you indicated when you registered. The score report is for your information only; you are not to submit it with your application for certification. Of course, as with any important document, you should keep a copy for your permanent records.

You may also access your test scores via the GACE Web site: unofficial test scores are posted on the Internet at 5 P.M. (EST) on the score report dates listed on the "Test Dates" page (*www.gace.nesinc.com/GA3_testdates.asp*). For each test date, the unofficial scores are kept on the Internet for approximately two weeks. You may only view these scores once during the posting period for security reasons.

Can I Retake the Test?

If you wish to retake a test, you may do so at any subsequent test administration. Please consult the GACE website (*www.gace.nesinc.com*) for information about test registration. The GACE website also includes additional information regarding test retakes and score reports.

Who Administers the Test?

The Georgia Professional Standards Commission (PSC) has contracted with Evaluation Systems to assist in the development and administration of the GACE. The GACE are aligned with state and national standards for educator preparation and with Georgia Performance Standards for the pre-kindergarten through twelfth-grade student curriculum.

For additional information, contact

GACE Program
Evaluation Systems
Pearson
P.O. Box 660
Amherst, MA 01004-9002
Phone: (800) 523-7064 or (413) 256-2894
Fax: (413) 256-7082 (Registration forms may not be transmitted by fax.)
Website: *www.gace.nesinc.com/*

For operator assistance, call 9 A.M. to 5 P.M. (EST) Monday through Friday, excluding holidays.

The Automated Information System is available 24 hours daily.

When Should I Take the Test?

Georgia law requires that teachers demonstrate mastery of basic skills, professional knowledge, and the content area in which they are specializing.

To receive information on upcoming administrations of the GACE Professional Pedagogy, consult the GACE website at *www.gace.nesinc.com*.

Do I Pay a Registration Fee?

To take the GACE, you must pay a registration fee. For information about the fees, log on to *www.gace.nesinc.com/GA3_testfees.asp*.

Can I Take the Test Online?

As of this writing, computer-based testing is not available for the GACE Professional Pedagogy assessment. For the latest update, go to *gace.nesinc.com/GA3_internet_based_testing.asp*.

How to Use This Book

When Should I Start Studying?

It is never too early to start studying for the GACE Professional Pedagogy tests. The earlier you begin, the more time you will have to sharpen your skills. Do not procrastinate! Cramming is not an effective way to study because it does not allow you the time you need to think about the content, review the subareas, and take the practice tests.

What Do the Review Sections Cover?

The targeted review in this book is designed to help you sharpen the basic skills you need to approach the GACE Professional Pedagogy tests, as well as provide strategies for attacking the questions.

Each subarea included in the Professional Pedagogy tests is examined in a separate chapter. The skills required for all areas are extensively discussed to optimize your understanding of what the examination covers.

Your life experience and your schooling have taught you most of the information you need to answer the questions on the test. Both should have provided you with the know-how to make important decisions about situations you will face as a teacher. The review sections in this book are designed to help you fit the information you have acquired into the competencies specified on the GACE. Your own background combined with the reviews provided here will give you an excellent springboard for passing the examination.

Studying for the Test

With this book in hand, the first step to effective test preparation is to find a good place to study:

1. Is your study area available whenever you are? Is it free from interruptions and distractions (no e-mail, no cell phone, no TV, no radio, no kids)?

2. Do you have everything you need (pen, pencil, highlighter, something to drink, something to eat, paper, etc.)?

3. Is there a desk or table available to work at? (The bed is absolutely out!)

4. Is the chair comfortable?

5. Is there enough light?

6. Is it warm or cool enough?

Once you've settled on an acceptable study area, you can focus on *how* to study:

1. Don't memorize.

2. If possible, study with a partner who is taking the same test. Review and discuss the material aloud—verbalization promotes learning.

3. If no partner is available, talk out loud to yourself! No, you're not crazy; remember, verbalization promotes learning.

4. Look for the interrelation between concepts in this guide.

5. Focus on understanding concepts, not remembering facts.

6. Master the concepts, not just a fuzzy understanding.

7. Start studying well in advance of the test—for these tests, four to six weeks is best.

8. Study everyday for a set period (one or two hours per day should be sufficient).

9. Begin each day's study early enough in the evening (or day) so you aren't exhausted when you start.

As mentioned earlier in the chapter, the Professional Pedagogy tests consist of 60 multiple-choice questions each and constructed-response questions. When taking the practice tests, use the following guidelines so that you will be familiar enough with them to apply them on the real test day:

Tips for Answering Multiple-Choice Questions

1. Read all of the possible answers for the multiple-choice question before selecting your answer.

2. On the practice tests (and in the test booklet on test day), cross out those answers that are clearly not correct. This helps you visually narrow down your choices.

3. Look for two answer choices that are opposites. One of them is most likely to be the correct answer.

4. Look for hints to the correct answer from other parts of the test. The correct answer choice might be part of another question. This is why it is often a good idea to read or at least look over the entire test when you first begin.

5. Look for answers that use language found in this study guide. Familiar language usually points to the correct answer.

6. Don't change your initial answer unless you are absolutely sure that another answer is correct.

7. Underline the important words in each question. This will help you answer what is being asked rather than what you think is being asked.

Tips for Answering Constructed-Response Questions

1. Begin with an outline of your response to the question.

2. KISS: Keep It Simple Silly! Answer the question in the simplest, most straightforward manner.

3. Answer the question that is asked. Do not engage in flights of fantasy under the assumption that you can baffle the test evaluators with brilliance.

4. Write legibly and use good grammar and standard English. Avoid slang, idiomatic expressions, and acronyms.

Time-Management Tips and General Suggestions

1. Pace yourself. Do not spend too much time on any one question. This is especially true for the essay questions. Leave yourself sufficient time to write the essays. Only you know how long that takes.

2. Answer the easiest questions first.

3. If you don't know an answer, skip the question and return to it at the end of the test. Do not leave any blanks. If you have no clue, just guess because there is no additional penalty for incorrect answers.

Now, let's get started. Each chapter of this book will correspond to a particular competency. Chapter 1 will be Competency 1, Chapter 2 will be Competency 2, and so forth. Take your time! And take control of the preparation process.

When you take the practice tests, simulate the conditions of the actual test as closely as possible. Turn off your television and radio, and sit down at a table in a quiet room, free from distraction. On completing a practice test, score it and thoroughly review the explanations to the questions you answered incorrectly; however, do not review too much at any one time. Concentrate on one problem area at a time by reviewing the question and explanation, and by studying the review in this guide until you are confident that you have mastered the material.

Keep track of your scores so you can gauge your progress and discover general weaknesses in particular sections. Give extra attention to the reviews that cover your areas of difficulty so you can build your skills in those areas. Many have found the use of study or note cards very helpful for this review.

How Can I Use My Study Time Efficiently?

Some people set aside a certain number of hours every morning to study, while others prefer to study at night before going to sleep. Other people study off and on during the day—for instance, while waiting for a bus or during a lunch break. Only you can determine when and where your study time will be most effective. Be consistent and use your time efficiently. Work out a study routine and stick to it.

The following study schedule allows for thorough preparation for the GACE Professional Pedagogy tests. The course of study presented here is seven weeks, but you can condense or expand the timeline to suit your personal schedule. It is vital that you adhere to a structured plan and set aside ample time each day to study. The more time you devote to studying, the more prepared and confident you will be on the day of the test.

Study Schedule

Week 1	After having read this first chapter to understand the format and content of this exam, take the first set of practice tests. The scores will indicate your strengths and weaknesses. Make sure you simulate real exam conditions when you take the tests. Afterward, score them and review the explanations, especially for questions you answered incorrectly.
Week 2	Review the explanations for the questions you missed, and review the appropriate chapter sections. Useful study techniques include highlighting key terms and information, taking notes as you review each section, and putting new terms and information on note cards to help retain the information.
Weeks 3 and 4	Reread all your note cards, refresh your understanding of the competencies and skills included on the exam, and review any college textbooks and notebooks you might have. You might want to review any troublesome material with an experienced teacher. This is also the time to consider any other supplementary materials that your counselor or the Georgia Department of Education suggests. Review the GACE website at *www. gace.nesinc.com.*
Week 5	Begin to condense your notes and findings. A structured list of important facts and concepts, based on your note cards and the GACE Professional Pedagogy competencies, will help you thoroughly review for the test. Review the answers and explanations for any questions you missed.
Week 6	Have someone quiz you using the note cards you created. Take the second set of practice tests, adhering to the time limits and simulated test-day conditions.
Week 7	Using all your study materials, review areas of weakness revealed by your score on the second set of practice tests. Then retake sections of the practice tests as needed.

The Day of the Test

Before the Test

On the morning of the test, be sure to dress comfortably so you are not distracted by being too hot or too cold while taking the test. Plan to arrive at the test center early. This will allow you to collect your thoughts and relax before the test and will also spare you the anguish that comes with being late. You should check your GACE Registration Bulletin to find out what time to arrive at the test center.

What to Bring

Before you leave for the test center, make sure that you have your admission ticket. This ticket lists your test selection, test site, test date, and reporting time.

You must also bring personal identification that includes one piece of current, government-issued identification, in the name in which you registered, bearing your photograph and signature, and one additional piece of identification (with or without a photograph). If the name on your identification differs from the name in which you are registered, you must bring official verification of the change (e.g., marriage certificate, court order).

If for any reason you do not have proper identification or your admission ticket, you will need to report immediately and directly to the Information Table at the test site. You may be required to complete additional paperwork, which may reduce your available testing time.

You must bring several sharpened No. 2 pencils with erasers, because none will be provided at the test center. If you like, you can wear a watch to the test center. However, you cannot wear one that makes noise, because it might disturb the other test takers. Dictionaries, textbooks, notebooks, calculators, cell phones, beepers, PDAs, scratch paper, listening and recording devices, briefcases, or packages are not permitted. Drinking, smoking, and eating during the test are prohibited.

You may bring a water bottle into the testing room, as long as it is clear without a label but with a tight lid. During testing, you will have to store your bottle under your seat.

Security Measures

As part of the identity verification process, your thumbprint will be taken at the test site. Thumbprints will be used only for the purpose of identity verification. If you do not provide a thumbprint, you will not be allowed to take the test. No refund or credit of any kind will be given. This thumbprint does not take the place of the complete fingerprint set requirement for Georgia teacher certification.

Enhanced security measures, including additional security screenings, may be required by test-site facilities. If an additional screening is conducted, only screened persons will be admitted to the test site. If you do not proceed through the security screening, you will not be allowed to test and you will not receive a refund or credit of any kind.

Late Arrival Policy

If you are late for a test session, you may not be admitted. If you are permitted to enter, you will not be given any additional time for the test session. You will be required to sign a statement acknowledging this. If you arrive late and are not admitted, you will be considered absent and will not receive a refund or credit of any kind. You will need to register and pay again to test at a future administration.

Absentee Policy

If you are absent, you will not receive a refund or credit of any kind. You will need to register and pay again to test at a future administration.

During the Test

The GACE Professional Pedagogy assessment is given in one sitting, with no breaks. However, during testing, you may take restroom breaks. Any time that you take for restroom breaks is considered part of the available testing time. Procedures will be followed to maintain test security. Once you enter the test center, follow all the rules and instructions given by the test supervisor. If you do not, you risk being dismissed from the test and having your score canceled.

When all the materials have been distributed, the test instructor will give you directions for completing the informational portion of your answer sheet. Fill out the sheet carefully, because the information you provide will be printed on your score report.

Once the test begins, mark only one answer per question, completely erase unwanted answers and marks, and fill in answers darkly and neatly.

Test-Taking Tips

By following the seven suggestions listed here, you can become more relaxed about taking the GACE, as well as other tests:

Tip 1. Stay calm and, as mentioned earlier, pace yourself. By using this book and studying effectively, you have become comfortable with the format of the GACE. You have simulated the test a number of times. Feel confident in the knowledge that all your preparation has boosted your chances of doing well.

Tip 2. Read all the possible answers. Just because you think you have found the correct response, do not automatically assume that it is the best answer. Read through each choice to be sure that you are not making a mistake by jumping to conclusions.

Tip 3. Use the process of elimination. Go through each answer to a question and eliminate as many of the answer choices as possible. If you can eliminate two answer choices, you have given yourself a better chance of getting the item correct, because only two choices are left from which to make your guess. Do not leave an answer blank; it is better to guess than not to answer a question on the GACE test because there is no additional penalty for incorrect answers.

Tip 4. Place a question mark in your answer booklet next to the answers you guessed, and then recheck them later if you have time.

Tip 5. Work quickly and steadily. You will have four hours to complete the test(s), so the amount of time you spend will depend upon whether you take both Professional Pedagogy tests in one test session. Taking the practice tests in this book will help you learn to budget your precious time.

Tip 6. Learn the directions and format of the test. This not only will save time but also will help you avoid anxiety (and the mistakes caused by being anxious).

Tip 7. When taking the multiple-choice portion of the test, be sure that the answer oval you fill in corresponds to the number of the question in the test booklet. The multiple-choice test is graded by machine, and marking one wrong answer can throw off your answer key and your score. Be extremely careful.

A test of this nature (a career-maker) is bound to create test anxiety. Here are some tips for keeping your nerves in check:

1. Study consistently, and use the tips mentioned in this chapter to gain a sense of mastery and confidence.

2. Use the power of positive thinking. Don't even consider failure; as you study, concentrate on how high your score will be as a result of your diligent preparation.

3. Do something to relax the night before the test. Go to a movie, eat well, and get to sleep early.

4. Eat a light breakfast or lunch prior to the test, and stay away from junk food.

5. Breathe slowly and deeply (don't hyperventilate!) during the test and maintain a can-do attitude.

6. Don't panic when others finish and leave the test room. There are lots of reasons for people to leave early! Take the time you need to do your best.

After the Test

When you finish your test, hand in your materials and you will be dismissed. Then go home and relax—you deserve it!

Competency 1

Understand human development, factors that
affect development, and how to apply this
understanding to promote student learning

Human Development

In order to successfully understand human development, we must examine the theories of Jean Piaget, Lawrence Kohlberg, Benjamin Bloom, and Erik Erikson.

Piaget's Cognitive Development Theory

Piaget's theory of cognitive development classifies children's psychological development into stages based on age. Piaget argued that in order to learn, children must be psychologically ready.

Piaget's Stages of Cognitive Development

> **Sensorimotor** (Birth to 2 years): In this first stage, children begin to differentiate themselves from objects. They recognize themselves as agents of action and begin to act intentionally, as when a child pushes a button to make a toy play a sound. Additionally, children in this stage begin to understand object permanence, realizing that things still exist even when they are no longer experienced.

> **Preoperational** (2 to 7 years): This stage is characterized by language development. The children learn to represent concepts through words and images. Children in this stage have difficulty taking on the viewpoints held by others. Children tend to be egocentric and classify objects by a single characteristic.

Concrete operational (7 to 11 years): Children in this stage can think logically about concepts. Unlike those in the preoperational stage, children who have reached the concrete operational stage can classify objects by multiple features and put them in order following a single characteristic (such as weight or size).

Formal operational (11 years and older): Adolescents and adults in this stage think logically about abstract concepts. They can form hypotheses and test hypotheses through systematic processes. Ideological issues and abstract thinking, such as concerns about the future, are characteristic of this stage.

Kohlberg's Moral Reasoning Theory

Kohlberg applied and expanded Piaget's concepts to "moral development." He believed that what he called moral reasoning evolved through three major phases, each containing two stages:

Preconventional level: The child is responsive to cultural concepts of right and wrong. Stage 1. *Punishment and obedience:* Physical punishment or rewards determine what is good or bad. Stage 2. *Instrumental-relativist:* Right is what satisfies one's own needs. Deals can be made.

Conventional level: The values of one's family or group are "good" regardless of consequences. Stage 3. *Interpersonal relationships:* Living up to expectations of family and community is "good." Stage 4. *Law and Order:* Living by the fixed rules of society is "good." Doing one's duty is "right."

Postconventional level: The child defines what is right or moral independently of authority or groups. Stage 5: *Social Contract:* What is "right" has been defined and agreed to by the individual independent members of society. Stage 6: *Universal principles:* "Right" is defined by an individual's social consciousness, according to that individual's chosen ethical principles.

Bloom's Taxonomy

The cognitive domain, described by Dr. Benjamin Bloom, is one of the best-known educational theories. He classified the forms and levels of learning into domains of learning. Bloom's theory asserts that a person cannot reach higher levels of the taxonomy until the lower levels have been achieved. Each level of the taxonomy embodies certain skills:

Knowledge: The ability to recall data or information

Understanding: The ability to comprehend the meaning, translation, and interpretation of instructions and problems

Application: The ability to use a concept in a new situation or the unprompted use of an abstraction

Analysis: The ability to separate material or concepts into component parts so that the organizational structure may be understood; being able to distinguish between facts and inferences

Synthesis: The ability to build a structure or pattern from diverse elements with an emphasis on creating a new meaning or structure

Evaluation: The ability to make judgments about the value of ideas or materials

The pyramid of Bloom's Taxonomy (see Figure 1.1) helps us see how the different levels of learning fit together. The pyramid's base, *Knowledge*, requires simply the knowing of facts. However, to take learning further, a person must fully *understand* the knowledge that is obtained, have the ability to *apply* it to different situations, to *analyze* its individual parts, and note how it can be *synthesized* or changed to create new meaning. Finally, the value of that knowledge must be *evaluated*.

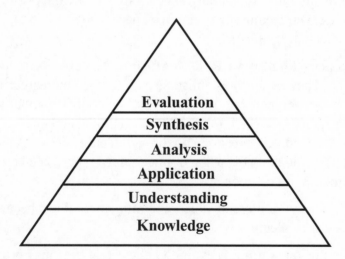

Figure 1.1   Bloom's Taxonomy

Erikson's Theory of Development

Erikson's theory of development is based on the belief that growth is a combination of physical, psychological, and cultural experiences. He argued that human development is a cumulative result of life experiences, including relationships, successes, and failures. He organized his theory of development into eight stages that extend from birth to death:

Birth to 1 year – Trust vs. Mistrust: Babies learn either to trust or to mistrust that others will care for their basic needs, including nourishment, sucking, warmth, cleanliness, and physical contact. Their focus is on motherly love and the senses of vision, hearing, and touch. If babies receive these things through this phase, then they come out of it thinking life is okay and have confidence about where they are going. However, if these needs are not met, babies emerge from this phase frustrated, with feelings of worthlessness and mistrust.

1 to 3 years – Autonomy vs. Shame and Doubt: Children learn either to be self-sufficient in many activities, including toileting, feeding, walking, and talking, or to doubt their own abilities. When children are shamed in this stage, it generates feelings of doubt and low self-esteem.

3 to 6 years – Initiative vs. Guilt: Children want to undertake many adultlike activities. Sometimes, they overstep the limits set by parents and as a result feel guilty. We see children copy adults and role-play in order to be more like the adults in their life.

7 to 11 years – Industry vs. Inferiority: Children easily learn to be competent. School and other social outlets begin to become the priority, replacing family. However, feelings of rejection by peers can result in feelings of inferiority and a lack of confidence.

Adolescence – Identity vs. Role Confusion: Adolescents try to figure out, "Who am I?" They begin to establish sexual, ethnic, and career identities that are separate from their family. They are often confused about what roles to play in the future and which roles will cause conflict and unease. Erikson also theorized that adolescents often go through identity crises. According to Erikson (1968), the identity diffusion or uncertainty experienced by most adolescents has four major components:

1. Intimacy: Adolescents fear commitment to others because it may involve a loss of identity.

2. Diffusion of time: They don't believe that time may bring change and yet have a strong fear that it might.

3. Diffusion of industry: Adolescents have either an inability to concentrate or direct a strong effort toward a single activity.

4. Negative identity: They are hostile about following the role seen correct by their families or community.

Young Adulthood – Intimacy vs. Isolation: Young adults begin to seek love and companionship with another person at this stage. However, if not successful, they may become isolated from others.

Middle Adulthood – Generativity vs. Stagnation: Middle-age adults focus on productive, meaningful work and raising a family. Alternately, they may enter this phase and become stagnant and inactive because of past failures.

Late Adulthood – Integrity vs. Despair: Older adults try to make sense out of their lives, either seeing life as a meaningful whole or despairing at goals never reached and questions never answered.

Factors Affecting Development

The following section highlights the required skills (in italics) of Competency 1 that relate to factors affecting human development. This review will give you a better understanding of these factors and how to apply your understanding to promote student learning.

Recognize the wide range of developmental variation among students at a given age or grade level and identify instructional practices that are responsive to developmental variation among students.

Human growth and development is a vast field of study that includes physical, mental, emotional, moral, and social developmental stages. No two students develop at the same rate, or with the same outcome, which means every classroom holds a fairly varied range of developmental stages. As educators, we must be familiar with these stages so that we can understand where our students exist on the developmental spectrum and what we can expect. Once we have this understanding, we can better deal with the diversity.

The next three required skills for Competency 1 are as follows:

Demonstrate knowledge of ways in which development in any one domain (e.g., cognitive, linguistic, social, affective, moral, artistic, physical) may affect development in other domains.

Demonstrate knowledge of major concepts and theories of human development (e.g., intellectual, linguistic, social, emotional, moral, physical).

Recognize characteristics and behaviors of students that are indicative of intellectual, linguistic, social, emotional, moral, and physical development.

All children experience these developmental changes simultaneously, but the rate at which they progress through them varies. For example, a student may be advanced in his cognitive development but less mature in terms of his social development. As a result, the student is highly intelligent but lacks the social skills to be accepted by his peers. Or perhaps a child may be developing faster physically than mentally. In this case, the child will look older than she acts. As educators, we need to remember that these situations exist, and take them into consideration when teaching. We can do this by accentuating the positive characteristics of our students and working on the underdeveloped areas on an individual basis. We must teach through a developmental approach, where we assess our students' levels of growth and plan a strategy that would best help them.

> *Identify developmentally appropriate instructional strategies, approaches, and learning opportunities for students.*

The ages of 6 through 9 are labeled the years of middle childhood. During this stage, children's large muscles are more developed than their small muscles. They can bounce a ball and run, but it is often difficult to do both at the same time. We see a large variance in the size and abilities of children in this age group. Their size and abilities will affect the way they get along with others, how they feel about themselves, and how they act. In this stage, children learn to use their small muscle skills such as handwriting. They use their large muscle skills, such as the ones they use to jump rope, as well. We must remember that this is a time of incredible growth, both mentally and physically, and need to allow our students time to rest periodically.

Cognitive development in the middle childhood years centers upon learning the concepts and skills valued by our culture, specifically reading, writing, and math skills. These are then built upon to promote more advanced learning. Students adopt planning skills and gain an understanding of actions and consequences. They learn that other people have different views, opinions, and knowledge.

> *Recognize the effects that peer interactions inside and outside of the classroom may have on student development, learning, and success in school, and identify strategies for addressing peer-related issues in the classroom.*

The social development of middle childhood begins when children begin to separate from their parents. Obviously, once they reach school age, children have more freedom than they did when they were toddlers. However, this freedom comes with more responsibility. Parents are partially replaced by teachers, coaches, camp counselors, and other adults. Because of this, children are presented with the opportunity to experience different morals, ideas, and values. Also, the influence of peers begins to play an important role. Children have the opportunity to make friends and learn how to navigate the dynamics of a social group. Children in this stage are gearing up for adolescence, and we must help them form a solid foundation on which to stand.

Adolescence is marked by the onset of puberty and can span all ages of the teenage years. We also see children younger than 13 and older than 19 who are pubescent. Hormones initiate the marked growth spurts and the development of primary and secondary sex characteristics. Usually girls begin experiencing these changes earlier than boys. With this incredible period of growth comes the awkwardness, moody behavior, and changes in eating habits that fit the stereotypical teenage mold. Students in this phase of life put much more value on their peer relationships than on their familial relationships. Status in their social group takes priority over school, family, church, and so on. Educators must keep in mind the social nature of adolescents and provide educational experiences that include communal learning.

> *Recognize how factors in the home and community (e.g., family expectations and involvement; cultural, linguistic, and socioeconomic background; availability of community resources; community issues) may affect student development and readiness to learn.*

As teachers, we need to provide our students with an environment in which they feel physically and emotionally comfortable, and give them the support they need to develop intellectually and socially. Students enter our classrooms from a diverse assortment of situations. Depending on cultural, familial, or communal expectation, our students' development and learning readiness will vary. Socioeconomic factors such as income and housing will influence which needs are met, as well as which direction our students will go in life. Each child's unique situation determines how he or she will develop and grow, and we must be willing to factor-in strategies to help them learn.

> *Analyze the effects of classroom factors (e.g., grouping practices, teacher expectations, teacher-student interactions) on students' self-concepts and learning.*

Whether we like it or not, our expectations of our students play a role in determining their success or failure. We hold that power, and we must use it well. Students pick up on the signals we give, and can tell if we think they cannot keep up. If we convey the message that all of our students are worthwhile, capable learners, then we can breed an environment of learning. Grouping students according to their achievements or the lack thereof is one way educators communicate failure. Students who see that they are in a low-achieving group often become victims of a self-fulfilling prophecy. Conversely, students whose teacher conveys high expectations often live up to these standards. Studies have shown that positive teachers with high expectations can make a difference in their students' learning potential.

Sample Questions for Competency 1

1. Billy has been caught stealing in your fifth-grade classroom. This has happened frequently before. Which of the following is the most likely cause of this behavior?

    A. Billy might possibly be emotionally disturbed.

    B. Billy needs the items he's stealing.

    C. Billy is in a normal stage of development.

    D. Billy is being taught to steal at home.

2. What aspect of development is most significant in children between 18 months and 30 months of age?

    A. Socialization skills

    B. Language skills

    C. Potty training

    D. Identity

3. Kohlberg's theory of moral development is useful to classroom teachers as they examine expectations of their students' ability to

    A. behave appropriately toward their peers.

    B. perform on standardized tests of ability.

    C. use language appropriately.

    D. think abstractly.

4. You've just learned that Johnny has been assigned to your classroom for the coming school year. Johnny's big brother was in your class last year, and you found him to be academically struggling. Johnny's teacher of last year mentions in the faculty room that Johnny's parents are difficult to deal with. Which of the following would be an appropriate response to this situation?

    A. You prepare for the worst and seat Johnny near your desk.

    B. You immediately begin to dread Johnny being in your class.

    C. You prepare to treat Johnny with high expectations and anticipate you will have a good year together.

    D. You ask if Johnny can be transferred to someone else's class.

5. You are going to use cooperative learning for the first time with your class. In creating the groups, you decide

    A. to allow students to select their own groups.

    B. to put all the students with behavior problems in one group so you can keep an eye on them.

    C. to create groups balanced by ability and learning style.

    D. to have students draw group numbers from a hat.

Answers

1. **A**

2. **B**

3. **A**

4. **C**

5. **C**

Competency 2

Understand learning processes, factors that affect student learning, and how to apply this knowledge to promote student development and learning

Learning Processes

In this section, we address the first of the Competency 2 required skills:

> *Demonstrate knowledge of how students construct and assimilate knowledge and develop new skills, including recognizing various types of learning strategies (e.g., rehearsal, elaboration, organization, and metacognition) and the roles of these strategies in promoting student learning.*

Learning is the process through which people acquire a new knowledge or skill, or change in attitude or behavior. Learning is acquired through either classical or operant conditioning.

Classical conditioning, as illustrated by the famous experimentation of Ivan Pavlov, refers to a learned reflexive response to stimuli. In Pavlov's experiments, dogs immediately began to drool at the sound of a bell because they had been conditioned to associate the sound of the bell with the arrival of a meal. In school, the ringing of the bell causes those lingering in the halls to rush to a classroom!

Operant conditioning, a theory developed by B. F. Skinner, focuses on the reward or punishment response to a behavior. Desirable behaviors result in a reward; undesirable behaviors result in a negative consequence. For example, a teacher might reward students' good behavior by allowing extra time at recess, or might institute a silent lunch period (a negative consequence) when students talk too much in the hallway.

Learning theories fall into three main categories: behaviorism, cognitivism, and constructivism.

Behaviorism stresses the importance of having a behavior reinforced by someone, other than the student, to shape or control what is learned. When teachers use drill and practice to teach math and reading skills they are employing the theory of behaviorism.

Cognitivism focuses on what is going on inside the student's mind. Learning is seen as a change in the student's way of thinking, understanding, or feeling. Jean Piaget's stages of development are a major part of the foundation of cognitivism. Cognitivism incorporates rehearsal, elaboration, and organizational strategies, as well as metacognition.

> **Rehearsal strategies** involve the repetition of concepts to be remembered. This is a good learning strategy for words and terms; however, deeper cognitive learning requires more than simple repetition.

> **Elaboration strategies** include various memory tasks, and activities such as summarizing, paraphrasing, and selecting main ideas from texts. Elaboration strategies result in deeper processing of the material and better comprehension than simple rehearsal strategies.

> **Organizational strategies** also help with comprehension. Note-taking, outlining, and concept mapping can help the student make connections between content elements.

> **Metacognition** is the awareness of our thinking processes and how we regulate them. This concept pertains to the way students plan out how they are going to learn, assess what they are learning, and decide if they need more clarification of the concept they have learned.

Constructivism, the third category of learning, defines learning as a process whereby students build new knowledge on top of their existing knowledge. There are two main concepts to constructivism:

- All knowledge is based on what it means to the individual learner.
- We must focus on the learner, not the subject matter.

Factors Affecting Student Learning

This section highlights the next required skill of Competency 2:

> *Demonstrate knowledge of factors that affect student learning (e.g., learning styles and preferences, prior knowledge and experience, developmental readiness) and how to modify instruction to meet student learning needs.*

This review will give you a better understanding of these factors and how to apply your understanding to promote student development and learning.

Principles of Learning The following principles are basic to classroom learning:

Readiness: Students learn best when they are physically and emotionally ready to learn. They do not learn well if they see no reason or relevance for learning or if their basic needs have not been met.

Exercise: Students tend to remember things better when they are encouraged to repeat them and practice them. However, as teachers, we must not allow our students to fall prey to tedium. Games, computer programs, and fun classroom activities can help students gain the practice they need without drudgery.

Effect: Positive instruction creates a better learning environment and motivates students to continue the learning process. Students respond better to a positive, upbeat environment than to a negative one. This calls for the teacher to use smiles, verbal approval, and active encouragement, without being condescending. Furthermore, the teacher can comment on the student's innate feelings of pride, accomplishment, understanding, ability, and skill.

Intensity: Students benefit from interactive, exciting classroom experiences rather than those that are passive and boring. Energy, spontaneity, and creativity keep students interested.

Recency: Things most recently learned are best remembered. This means that we need to reinforce previously taught concepts by bringing them back to the forefront, especially if they are prerequisite knowledge for a new lesson.

Primacy: A student's first impression is perhaps the strongest. This is why it is critical that we teach a concept the right way the first time, and build a strong foundation for what is to come.

Gardner's Theory of Multiple Intelligences

Howard Gardner's theory of multiple intelligences is based on his assertion that all people possess basic, albeit diverse, functions of learning. It is the strength of the individual's functions and how well the individual uses them that determines his or her level of learning. Gardner has identified seven distinct categories of learning, and we can use this list as a foundation for creating lessons that will appeal to all types of learners.

Spatial-Visual: People who are strong spatial-visual learners think in terms of physical space. They like to draw, perhaps doodling while listening to a lecture, and can easily get distracted by daydreams. Using art or verbal imagery can help these students. Tools to help in their learning process include pictures, models, graphics, charts, photographs, three-dimensional models, video, and multimedia.

Linguistic: Linguistic learners are those who have highly developed auditory skills and often think in words. They are sensitive to the meaning and order of words and thrive on activities such as reading, word games, and constructing poetry or stories. Helpful teachers encourage these students by allowing them to say and see words, and by reading books together. Helpful learning tools include computers, multimedia, books, games, and lecture.

Bodily-Kinesthetic: Kinesthetic learners need to use their bodies and manipulate objects in order to learn most effectively. They have a superior sense of body awareness, and like movement and constructing things. Physical activity and equipment, manipulating real objects with hands-on contact, role-playing and drama are helpful tools with which to teach these learners.

Musical: These learners possess sensitivity to rhythm, pitch, melody, and sound. They love music, but they are also sensitive to sounds in their environments. They may study better with music in the background. Putting lessons into lyrics, speaking rhythmically, tapping out time, using musical instruments, and multimedia are all helpful tools for these students.

Logical-Mathematical: Reasoning, calculating, and identifying patterns are skills that come easily to logical-mathematical learners. They tend to think conceptually, abstractly, and are able to see patterns and relationships in the world. These learners need to understand whole concepts before they can deal with details. Helpful teaching tools include experiments, puzzles, logic games, investigations, and mysteries.

Interpersonal: Interpersonal learners are skilled at understanding and interacting with others. These students learn through interaction and tend to have many friends. They can be taught through group activities, seminars, and dialogues. Helpful teaching tools include conferences and discussions, time and attention from the instructor, writing, and e-mail communication.

Intrapersonal: People who value most strongly an understanding of their own interests and goals are intrapersonal learners. Although these learners may be in tune with their inner feelings, they may shy away from others. Independent study and introspection along with books, journals, and time to reflect are helpful ways to help these students learn.

An eighth form of intelligence has recently been added to the original list: **naturalistic intelligence.** It is characterized by a person's ability to relate and interpret nature.

Additional Competency 2 Skills

Recognize how characteristics of a diverse student population, including students at different developmental levels, affect learning processes and how to modify instruction to meet students' learning needs.

The diversity of today's classrooms presents a challenge for teachers. We must use assessment tools to identify patterns of physical, social, and academic development in our students. Then we need to identify strategies and factors that will encourage achievement for students at all of the various ability levels present in our classrooms. We then must design our lessons around the different developmental levels and individual abilities of our learners.

Demonstrate knowledge of strategies for helping students build meaning (e.g., making connections between students' existing knowledge and new concepts, relating learning to students' lives, engaging students in authentic learning experiences) and develop higher-level thinking and reasoning skills.

Now that we understand how diverse learners collect and process data, we can develop teaching strategies that work. Robert Marzano, a noted expert on teaching, and the author of the book *Classroom Instruction That Works*, (with Debra Pickering and Jane Pollock), has developed nine essential concepts for teaching:

1. Identifying similarities and differences: We can teach students how to break down concepts into categories of similar and dissimilar characteristics. This

enables students to grasp complex problems by analyzing them in a simpler format. Examples of this include comparing and contrasting activities such as Venn diagrams and charts.

2. Summarizing and note taking: We reinforce comprehension skills when we ask students to take notes on a concept and then summarize it. By restating the idea in their own words, students are better able to understand it.

3. Reinforcing effort and providing recognition: We can build student confidence and foster a desire to learn when we show the connection between effort and achievement. Praising students and giving recognition for accomplishments builds desirable behavior.

4. Homework and practice: Research shows that students learn better through practice and repetition. Homework should be grade appropriate and student focused.

5. Nonlinguistic representations: Students tend to grasp concepts better when they can physically see them. Models, symbols, and movement help student understanding.

6. Cooperative learning: Small-group learning builds social skills, grows accountability, and appeals to students' desire for communication and socialization.

7. Setting objectives and providing feedback: Goals and objectives help students see where they are and where they are going in the learning process. Rubrics and timely feedback are important.

8. Generating and testing hypotheses: Students learn well from predicting hypothetical outcomes and then exploring the results. Higher-level skills such as critical and creative thinking and problem solving are enriched in this process.

9. Cues, questions, and advance organizers: We can help students by reinforcing their learning with concepts they have already learned. This information should be given before the lesson.

> *Analyze strategies for encouraging students to become independent thinkers and learners (e.g., by fostering students' critical-thinking, creative-thinking, and problem-solving skills by providing students with opportunities to make choices and pursue topics of interest) in order to reach learning goals.*

Rather than lecturing at our students, we can invigorate their learning experience and help them develop higher-level thinking skills by allowing them the opportunity to play a role in determining what they will learn. If we want students to cultivate proficient reasoning and problem-solving skills, we must be willing to give them the freedom to learn by engaging in authentic experiences rather than absorbing and regurgitating what they are taught. Using lesson strategies based on Gardner's theory of multiple intelligences and Marzano's nine essential concepts are the key to providing an authentic education.

> *Demonstrate knowledge of the various roles of teachers (e.g., facilitator, coach, direct instructor) and students (e.g., self-directed learner, collaborator, observer) in the instructional process and the effects of these roles on learning processes and outcomes.*

In addition to being teachers and students, participants in the classroom fulfill a variety of roles. Teachers are also coaches, support personnel, guides, and surrogate parents. Our students expect us to fill these roles and need us to be strong, guiding role models. We are no longer just lecturers on the stage. We are guides who are there to help our students become self-directed learners who can observe, think critically, collaborate with others, and pursue lifelong learning goals.

Sample Questions for Competency 2

1. Sally is having difficulty preparing for tests in your class. She has failed two exams despite "studying." What would you suggest for this third-grader as she prepares for the upcoming spelling test?

    A. Show her how to rehearse, using repetition. That is, have her repeat the word and its spelling 25 times.

    B. Tell her she is not studying hard enough, and remind her if she fails she will be left back.

    C. Immediately recommend her for special education evaluation.

    D. Let her mother know that she is failing.

2. According to Howard Gardner, a student who exhibits talents in perceiving visual images and imagined representations possesses which of the multiple intelligences?

    A. Bodily-Kinesthetic

    B. Logical-Mathematical

    C. Spatial

    D. Naturalist

3. Thomas and Sandra are both well-behaved and responsible students. Thomas can't seem to turn in a coherent notebook or write a decent lab report in your ninth-grade Life Science class. He does the experiments very well and when questioned gives excellent answers about what was done. Sandra has a comprehensive notebook and impeccable lab reports; her work in the lab is substandard; and she is often confused about the concepts being learned.

   A. Sandra must be having someone else do her notebook and lab reports.

   B. Thomas is just lazy. If he knows the answers, he's just not trying on the written work.

   C. Both Sandra and Thomas should stay after school where you can supervise the work they do on the labs, and the written work.

   D. Sandra and Thomas have different intelligences as noted by Howard Gardner. Perhaps they should be lab partners so they can complement each other.

4. What steps are important in the review of subject matter in the classroom?

   A. A rehearsal of the subject matter and a topic summary within the lesson

   B. A one-paragraph synopsis of the previous lesson and a review in writing at the end of the lesson

   C. A preview of the lesson, an in-depth discussion within the lesson, and a lesson-ending review

   D. A lesson-initiating review, the lesson topic, and a lesson-ending review

5. Recency is a concept that suggests the following strategy for our teaching:

   A. We need to be passionate about what we teach.

   B. We need to be upbeat and positive about what we teach.

   C. We need to reinforce previously taught concepts, especially if they are required prior knowledge.

   D. We need to be relevant in our teaching.

Answers

1. **A**

2. **C**

3. **D**

4. **D**

5. **C**

Competency 3

3

Understand student diversity, how to apply this knowledge to promote learning for all students, and how to foster students' appreciation of and respect for diversity within and beyond the classroom

Student Diversity

By understanding the unique differences of our students, we will be able to adapt our teaching methods to meet the learning needs of all students.

Our educational system is experiencing greater student diversity than ever before. Educators are being asked to accommodate student differences related to gender, ethnicity and culture, heritage, socioeconomics, and exceptionality. When dealing with such a diverse population of students, we must be willing to respect a variety of *value systems*.

A **value system** is a set of common beliefs held by members of a particular culture or segment of society. This set of beliefs is held up as true, right, and proper. However, another culture or segment of society can have a different value system and consider it true, right, and proper. This is where teachers must be accepting and knowledgeable.

The majority of teachers and school administrators in the United States reflect beliefs and behaviors that are characteristic of the white middle class. Yet, according to a 2002 study by the National Center for Education Statistics, approximately 41 percent of our classrooms have at least one English language learner (ELL) and 40 percent of our students are from culturally and linguistically diverse backgrounds. This evidence shows that our traditional ways of teaching, designed for students with a homogenous value system, are outdated.

While the traditional American value system may appeal to one segment of our students, we must examine and develop an understanding of others.

We will look now at several of our nation's minority groups and examine what makes them unique. This is information critical to the first two of the Competency 3 required skills:

> *Demonstrate awareness of different types of diversity (e.g., ethnic and cultural heritage, socioeconomic circumstances, gender, linguistic background, exceptionality) and their implications for teaching and learning.*
>
> *Recognize appropriate strategies for enhancing the teacher's own understanding of students' diverse background and needs (e.g., learning about students' families, cultural heritage, socioeconomic circumstances, gender, linguistic background, exceptionality) and their implications for teaching and learning.*

Cultural Diversity

Hispanic Students

Hispanic American students are Mexican, Puerto Rican, Cuban, Central or South American, or from other Spanish origins. They are also called Latinos, and their ancestral language is Spanish. The use of the Spanish language is very prevalent in the homes of today's Hispanic families, as students often have parents who speak very little English. The Hispanic American community is the fastest growing demographic group in the United States, but unfortunately, the dropout rate of Hispanic American students is second highest in the country. We must take very seriously our efforts to develop ways to insure our Hispanic American students receive a quality education so that many more will continue on in school and achieve academic success.

Understanding the Latino culture includes learning about their family relationships. Latino families are extremely loyal and supportive. A child's behavior reflects upon the family's honor, and parents tend to be very interested in their child's learning. However, quite often there is a language barrier between parents and educators, which makes it even more imperative that we find a way to reach them. Individual dignity is important to Latinos, and respect for authority is a valued quality. By applying our understanding of these components of the Hispanic American culture, we can develop a strategy for best serving this group of students.

Hispanic American children who come from vibrant, communicative homes need to feel welcome, supported, and enthused when they walk into our classrooms. Educators can begin to build relationships with these students by showing interest in their ethnicity and respecting their language and culture. Activities that allow the students to celebrate or bring recognition to Hispanic leaders and role models not only help the Hispanic students to feel a sense of pride about their origins, but also grow cultural tolerance in the non-Hispanic students. When there are challenges with language, allowing students extra time to reflect on a question before answering encourages them to try, and can foster self-confidence. When the students know that they are accepted as part of the classroom community, they can feel comfortable engaging in classroom activities.

In addition to demonstrating acceptance of the Hispanic American culture, educators need to build relationships with the students' families. It seems quite logical to incorporate familial bonds in the learning process. However, we often see educators shying away from reaching out to families because of lack of time or methods of communication. The communication barrier may also deter parents from contacting the teacher. In fact, some parents who have had bad school experiences of their own may not want anything to do with their child's teachers. Even with the enormous amount of work required and the obstacles of communication and misunderstandings, teachers can make a difference. Educators who see the opportunity to build relationships with families and reach out to the community can significantly increase their students' involvement.

African American Students

African Americans have origins in any of the African black racial groups. African American students tend to use animated language, talk simultaneously, and enjoy close proximity when communicating. Often, these children come from single-parent households, or perhaps a grandparent's household. In this kind of situation, teachers can think of themselves as a surrogate parent for the students. Incorporating the African American heritage into our lessons and activities is vital to establishing a sense of belonging for our African American students.

Coming from such a society-oriented community, African American students can benefit from cooperative learning opportunities. These students enjoy lively discussions, rapid intonation, rhythmic and figurative language, and analogies. Changes in our presentation and planning fresh activities can help keep interest levels high. Our African American students need to be taught relevant material that shows members of their community in successful and positive scenarios. Role models and mentors can be beneficial as well.

Asian American and Pacific Islander Students

Asian Americans have origins in East Asia, Southeast Asia, and the Indian subcontinent. Pacific Islanders have origins in Hawaii and the U.S Pacific territories of Guam, American Samoa, Palau, Micronesia, Melanesia, and the Philippines. These students are generally thought of as successful, conformist, intelligent, and high-achieving.

Asian Americans tend to maintain strong family ties, and they are very group-oriented. They are used to working as a group, for the common good of the group. This may cause difficulty when adjusting to the Western culture because of its emphasis on the individual. The Asian American/Pacific Islander cultures place a great deal of value on respect for elders, family responsibility, self-discipline, and scholarly learning. With an emphasis on deferred gratification, these students are taught to be introspective, thoughtful, and respectful. They may dislike attention directed at them and prefer to look away rather than make eye contact.

Asian American/Pacific Islanders tend to learn better in a well-structured environment. In addition, learning a few words of the students' native language demonstrates respect for and interest in them. Again, in these cases where there can be challenges with language, allow students extra time to reflect on a question before they have to answer. Having more time to translate in their heads can foster confidence.

In addition to working on communication skills, we can encourage these students to become more outspoken in class. We can help students understand that they may respectfully share their opinions in the school environment. Classroom activities such as role-playing and skits can help model desirable communication characteristics. Finally, we can encourage student involvement in clubs and activities for socializing, which not only helps build better communication skills but also addresses the need to build lasting friendships.

American Indian/Alaskan Native Students

The description of American Indian/Alaskan Native refers to a person having origins in any of the native or indigenous inhabitants of North America. There are approximately 500 different tribes in North America, speaking over 200 different languages. Talk about diversity!

Unfortunately, this group of students has the highest dropout rate in the U.S. public school system. Possible reasons for the high drop-out rate include:

- Poverty

- Lack of curricular relevance to the students' lives

- Students feel they are being forced to abandon their traditional customs

- Different learning styles from mainstream

- Lack of parental involvement in school

- Parents' negative memories of school experiences

As with previously discussed student groups, American Indian/Alaskan Native students want to feel included, respected, and understood in our classrooms. Teachers need to learn about their culture so they can attempt to understand their value system and how it differs from the mainstream American ways of thinking. We can provide a curriculum that fosters critical thought and social justice through creative activities and cultural elements. Like Asian American students, American Indian/Alaskan Native students may not choose to make eye contact, not as an act of defiance, but as an act of respect. We must also try to take into account their hesitancy to show academic competence, as they may not want to seem superior to others in their family or tribe.

Above all, all of our students need to be approached with sensitivity, sincerity, and respect to bolster their academic potential.

Tips for Teaching in Culturally Diverse Classrooms

- Educate yourself about your students' value systems.

- Become knowledgeable about the obscure differences in cultural behavior.

- Show sensitivity for students, their families, and their lifestyles.

- Build a trusting, supportive relationship with your students.

- Make the curriculum relevant to students' lives.

- Help students find an adult mentor, or be a mentor for them.

- Have high expectations for your students and express to them what you expect.

- Be culturally sensitive when developing classroom codes of conduct.

- Emphasize responsibility and respect.

- Maintain a working, supportive relationship with students' families.

Students with Disabilities

In addition to cultural diversity, educators are confronted with the task of teaching inclusion students who can have one of a myriad of physical or learning disabilities. Disabilities may include visual impairments, speech and language disorders, or mild learning or behavioral/neurological-based differences. A 2002 report from the U.S. Department of Education revealed that nearly 12 percent of students are enrolled in special education programs.

Editor's Note: The information on diversity is taken from 2021 course work at both Armstrong Atlantic State University, Savannah, and Savannah State University (an HBCU).

The next two Competency 3 required skills are particularly relevant to the teaching of students with disabilities:

> *Analyze strategies for planning and adapting instruction that is responsive to the characteristics, skills, interests, strengths, and needs of all students and for ensuring that all students participate to the greatest extent possible in classroom activities.*
>
> *Identify resources in the school and community for meeting individual needs and recognize appropriate strategies for facilitating student and family access to these resources.*

Neurological-Based Disabilities

Neurological-based disabilities typically affect students' ability to process information or remember what they have previously learned. Such disabilities are often treated with a variety of therapies, including medication, and educators must be aware of the symptoms and difficulties experienced by these students. It is also necessary to be able to recognize the side effects of the medicines taken by students. Here are some examples:

- **Attention-deficit hyperactivity disorder (ADHD)** is characterized by a short attention span and restlessness.

- **Affective disorders** affect a person's moods and feelings. A person with bipolar disorder, for example, fluctuates between feelings of mania and depression.

- **Anxiety disorders** involve feelings of fear and panic.

- **Posttraumatic stress disorder** is a type of anxiety disorder resulting from exposure to a traumatic event.

- **Conduct disorder** is characterized by repeated misbehavior such as rule breaking.

- **Oppositional-defiant disorder** is characterized by repeated, purposeful defiance and/or opposition to authority figures.

- **Autism spectrum disorders (ASD)** constitute a range of developmental deficits in communication skills, social interactions, and repetitive behaviors. Symptoms can be mild to severe, and each child with ASD manifests them differently.

- **Fetal alcohol spectrum disorders** are characterized by poor impulse control, lack of common sense, and poor judgment, all of which result in learning difficulties.

Learning Disabilities

Learning disabilities are disorders that disrupt the students' learning process. Such disorders may be subject or topic specific. Here are some examples:

- **Dyslexia** affects language processing.
- **Dyscalculia** affects learning basic math skills.
- **Dysgraphia** affects handwriting and spelling.
- **Dyspraxia** affects fine motor skills.

Educators must understand that learning disabilities can affect students who have average to above-average intelligence. With the right support and intervention, these students can adapt to their disability and thrive in school.

Inclusion

The Individuals with Disabilities Education Act of 1975 requires that students with disabilities have access to a free and appropriate education. In order to ensure these students are getting the opportunity to learn as much as possible, they are included in the mainstream classrooms when possible.

The concept of **inclusion** is threefold:

1. Students with special needs are placed in a regular classroom unless the nature of the disability is such that proper education in a regular classroom cannot be achieved.

2. Support services are provided to guarantee these students adapt.

3. General and special education services are coordinated to work together.

For teachers with inclusion students in their classroom, focusing on the individual student is a must. Teachers should work with special educators to develop individualized education programs (IEPs) for these students.

An IEP must include

- annual and short-term goals and objectives that are measurable and follow the general curriculum

- the services and modifications to the program that will allow the child to achieve set goals by participating in the regular and extra curriculum

- a schedule for the program of services, including a start date, location, frequency, and duration

- an explanation, if the student will not participate in regular classroom activities

- a description of any changes made to assessments

In addition to in-class strategies, we can help our students and their families by identifying school and community resources that can help meet their needs. Sources such as school counselors and mentor programs are designed to help students and their families adapt to their environment. In addition, educators can research community programs such as youth clubs, churches, libraries, and local colleges to find assistance. Internet searches can be helpful in locating help as well.

Additional Strategies

The number of our diverse students is growing quickly, and so is the level of concern that they get a fair and supportive education. As educators, we can be on the front lines fighting for these students and their families through fairness and acceptance. If we demonstrate respect for others, encourage interaction between diversities, and hold high expectations for all learners, we can call ourselves advocates for students of diversity. Hence, the final required skill for Competency 3:

Demonstrate knowledge of strategies for fostering students' understanding of and respect for diversity and for using the diversity in the classroom and the community to enhance learning for all students.

When it comes to understanding and respecting diversity, we can model the behavior we want reflected in our students. We must be specifically dedicated to keeping our classroom a safe, accepting environment. Here are some final tips for teaching in diverse classrooms:

- Recognize any of your own biases or stereotypes.

- Treat each student as an individual, and respect who they are.

- Refuse to allow any language patterns or case examples that exclude or demean any groups.

- Be aware of biased terminology.

- Ask students how they feel about the cultural climate in your classroom.

- Show confidence in the abilities of all your students; don't try to "protect" any group.

- Be evenhanded when praising students' good work.

- Whenever possible, select texts that use gender-neutral language and that are free of stereotypes.

- Do not assume all students will be familiar with cultural, literary, or historical references.

- Consider the possibility of unconventional schedules when assigning evening or weekend work.

- Host guest lecturers. Advise students to explore perspectives outside their own experiences. (Davis 1993)

- Emphasize the necessity of considering different viewpoints.

- Encourage students to form study groups outside of class.

Sample Questions for Competency 3

1. In a culturally diverse classroom it is imperative that the teacher

    A. be aware of any stereotypes or biases that they may have.

    B. be fair and treat all children exactly the same.

    C. avoid feelings of guilt in terms of how certain cultures have been treated in the past.

D. encourage students to form study groups that are similar in culture to avoid confusion.

2. Your eighth grade social studies class is an inclusion class with a wide variety of developmental and ability levels. How would you address the needs of all of your students?

A. Teach to the middle of the class, and use a bell curve to grade the students.

B. Teach to the least able students and do not curve the grades.

C. Use a variety of teaching strategies, and modify both instruction and evaluation based on the individual student.

D. Modify only as required by IEP; hold all students to high standards.

3. What is the goal of multicultural education?

A. Enable teachers to generalize across ethnic groups.

B. Encourage ethnic groups to adopt the practices of the dominant culture.

C. Identify students with Limited English Proficiency.

D. Provide all children with equality of opportunity.

4. An IEP must include

A. the names of the teachers that will be providing the services.

B. a plan for placing the student back into the mainstream classroom.

C. any suggestions made by parents.

D. annual short-term goals that are measurable.

5. According to a recent government study, what percent of U.S. public school students are enrolled in special education?

A. 40%

B. 20%

C. 12%

D. 5%

Answers

1. **A**

2. **C**

3. **D**

4. **D**

5. **C**

Competency 4

Understand how to establish a safe, inclusive, and positive learning environment that fosters learning, equity, and excellence

Learning Environment

The climate of the classroom must be safe, caring, and inclusive for all students if the learning environment is to be successful. Teachers are obligated to provide an emotionally and socially safe environment as well. Students must feel comfortable around the other students in the class in order to feel confident participating.

One skill needed to meet the requirements for Competency 4 is as follows:

> *Demonstrate knowledge of effective methods for creating a supportive learning community through the development of shared goals, experiences, and positive interactions (e.g., student-to-student, teacher-to-student).*

Student relationships have an enormous impact on the student learning environment. Students who do not have positive interactions with teachers or other students tend to become a problem to all students in the classroom. Having positive interactions creates an effective learning environment. It is essential for all students to have a positive relationship with other students—and especially with the teacher.

A method for creating a supportive learning environment is to develop shared goals that students and teachers agree on and that each feel are significant and important for the success of the classroom. Students with goals are more motivated, and they participate regularly by collaborating with other students.

Having common goals assures everyone that all involved are working to accomplish the same thing. There are fewer problems within the classroom environment when students and teachers are committed to common goals.

To have a successful goal-supportive learning community, the teacher should do the following:

- Set highly meaningful goals. The goals should be important to both the student and the teacher. If the goals are not important, students will have no desire to work toward attaining the goals that are set.

- Establish the methods for attaining the goals when setting them. Students and teachers should not only agree on the goals themselves but also on how to attain them.

Note that the resources to attain goals should be available, and no goal should be set if the resources needed to meet it are not readily available. In addition, all goals should be in line with all education objectives. The goals should be set so that they accomplish important educational objectives. The goals should be a part of the learning environment and used to provide positive relationships among students and between students and the teacher. Finally, goals should challenge and motivate students. The goals should be attainable, yet they should challenge the students and motivate them to work harder to be able to accomplish more.

> *Analyze strategies for promoting positive social interactions among students, facilitating conflict resolution, and encouraging students' adherence to ethical principles (e.g., honesty, academic integrity, self-respect, and respect for others, tolerance, personal responsibility).*

Successfully using this skill leads to having an environment that is safe for students to express themselves. It helps to motivate all students when the environment permits all students to participate in the classroom.

Having a classroom policy will create a safe and caring learning environment. If an environment feels safe to a student, he or she will be more likely to participate in class.

Some students may have difficulty participating because they feel uncomfortable with the spotlight on them. One option would be to have small groups so students do not have as many people watching and listening to them at one time. Students can also spend a few moments each day after class asking the teacher questions that they could not or would not ask during class. When the teacher makes a little effort to help those students, they will become more comfortable and can learn to participate just like the others.

Encouraging students' adherence to ethical principles is important. Students of all ages should receive an education in proper behavior, as well as in the academic and other school subjects they are taught each day. Many students do not receive enough discipline or do not receive proper discipline at home. For this reason, many students do not know how to behave all the time. It is up to the teacher to deal with this kind of student.

> *Demonstrate knowledge of strategies and procedures for establishing a safe, inclusive, and caring classroom climate that encourages students' active engagement, risk taking, and collaboration in learning.*

The teacher must use many different strategies to deal with many different students and many different situations. A teacher is sometimes left with a responsibility that is often neglected by parents. It is sometimes a teacher who has the greatest impact on a student's behavior. Having fair and well-defined classroom rules is usually the first strategy a teacher can use in the classroom environment.

GACE Tip

It is always helpful to have fair and easily understood classroom rules.

Rules both help to teach a student what is expected and encourage personal responsibility. When establishing a set of rules for a classroom, several things should be considered:

1. Students should be able to understand the rules. They must be written so that the student can understand the *entire* meaning of the rules, which means that they must be written with age-appropriate language.

2. The rules must be made so that the students can comply with them. A student acting in a reasonable manner should be able to adhere to the rules.

3. The rules must be fair and be applied to all students. A teacher should consider the age level of the students. The teacher should also consider social behavior and the environment when making rules.

4. It is important to state all the rules in a positive manner. Rules written positively encourage positive behavior and adherence to the rules.

5. The rules should reflect the needs and goals of the school and the classroom teacher. No classroom rule should contradict any established schoolwide or systemwide rules. The school's and teacher's philosophies should also be considered when classroom rules are made.

6. Consequences should be included with the rules. Consequences should be based on behavior and should be clear, just as individual rules are. The consequences should be reasonable and consistent with the behavior that constituted a breaking of the rule.

7. Students may give input when creating rules for the learning environment. Students who are encouraged to participate in making the rules often adhere to them much better. They have ownership of the rules that they create, which causes them to follow the rules better.

Every teacher must deal with the topic of conflict resolution. Some conflict is very simple, such as when one student takes a pencil from another student as a joke. Other conflict can be very severe, such as when two students fight because one student used a racial slur when referring to the other. Conflicts are very unpredictable. Because of their unpredictable nature, it is difficult to create rules and consequences for all conflicts. Students who are bullied or made fun of by others will not participate in class for fear of being picked on or laughed at. It is the teacher's responsibility to stop any actions by students to intimidate others.

The severity of the conflict should be considered when determining a consequence for the conflict. The punishment should fit the actions of the student involved in the conflict. Here are some strategies for resolving conflicts in the learning environment:

1. Gather information about what happened without making any accusations. Ask people in the vicinity what they may have seen or heard.

2. Allow each person involved to state his or her position. Allow everyone to state how they were affected by the incident.

3. Try to get each party to look at the incident from the viewpoint of the other party.

4. Ask each party to suggest how to resolve the conflict. Ask each side to brainstorm about how they can reach common ground and settle the conflict so they can prevent future problems.

5. Peers can be used to mediate a solution to the conflict. Each party should agree to have a third party mediate a solution to the conflict.

6. If the conflict still cannot be resolved, each party could agree to arbitration by *another* third party. This would be similar to mediation. A third party would hear both sides of the issue. They would then issue a decision that both sides must agree and comply with. Choosing to have an arbitrator would end the conflict. Either or both of the parties may not like the decision of the arbitrator, but the decision is final.

Recognize the benefits and limitations of various physical arrangements within the classroom and analyze strategies for organizing the physical environment to ensure accessibility and facilitate learning in various instructional contexts.

The physical arrangement of the classroom can have an effect on a student's learning. The arrangement of furniture, lighting, and even colors in the room can have a positive or negative effect on a student's ability to learn. A learning environment, when properly arranged, will provide safety and thus will be an effective environment for learning. Conversely, when the learning environment is improperly arranged, it can be very distracting to students. The classroom arrangement can help facilitate different types of learning, based on the goals of the teacher.

The design of the learning environment is an essential element in promoting student learning. A teacher choosing to emphasize small groups and other forms of collaboration would want to arrange students' desks to encourage this type of learning. When students are arranged as part of a group, they are encouraged simply through proximity

GACE Tip

Put considerable thought into the arrangement of students' desks.

to participate within the group. Collaboration is more natural and is encouraged when students are already in groups.

If the focus of the class and material is on demonstrations and presentations, then the teacher may choose a classroom design that has students facing in the direction of the presenter. This will usually be toward the front of the classroom. Just as daily lessons are unique, the design of the classroom is unique and should help to facilitate the goals of the teacher for the particular lesson. It may be necessary to change the classroom design regularly to match the needs of the lesson.

Any design for a classroom should be used to facilitate the types of learning being encouraged by the teacher and can be set up in any configuration. The teacher should arrange and use the physical environment of the classroom to accomplish the goals of the course.

Here are four strategies that may be used to develop a physical environment that will ensure a positive learning environment:

1. Choose a grouping to benefit the needs of the course. How to arrange student desks should be the first and most important decision when choosing an arrangement for the learning environment.

2. Ensure a safe arrangement in the classroom. The arrangement should be free from clutter, and students should be able to move throughout the classroom.

3. Temperature, lighting, and other elements should be controlled within the learning environment. Lighting is very important and should be effective throughout the space. Temperature, furnishings, and colors should enhance the learning environment and should not distract students in any way.

4. Furnishings within the learning environment, including student desks and chairs, should be comfortable and attractive. Having comfortable and attractive furnishings encourages student learning by making students want to be in the learning environment.

Sample Questions for Competency 4

1. At the beginning of the school year, a new student, Jorge, enters your class. He is also new to the school. He appears uncomfortable and doesn't readily enter into class activities. What can you do to help his situation?

    A. Give him extra work to do at home to help him catch up with the class.

    B. Have him join you and several outgoing youngsters to plan goals for an upcoming project.

    C. Call in his parents for an immediate consultation.

    D. Ask the guidance counselor for a review of his past record.

2. One of your students, Rebecca, doesn't seem to know the correct behavior to use in the lunchroom. She upsets a number of the other girls with her lack of social skills. What can you do?

    A. Create positive, age appropriate, and clearly understood rules for all to follow in the lunchroom.

    B. Call in her guardians and tell them they have to teach Rebecca some manners.

C. Scold Rebecca for her lack of respect for her classmates.

D. Prohibit her from sitting with the other girls.

3. You take great joy in creating a positive environment in your classroom. However, the one rule you should NOT follow is:

A. Use the physical environments to accomplish the goals of your class.

B. Once your room is set up, keep it exactly the same all year.

C. Make use of seating to facilitate small groups and other forms of collaboration.

D. Face the students in the direction of the presenter.

4. You are developing rules for your fourth grade class. Which of the following would NOT be part of your consideration?

A. Rules must be simple enough to be understood by all of your students.

B. Rules should be written in the negative voice so that all will understand clearly what they may not do.

C. Rules must also reflect the goals of the school.

D. There should be reasonable consequences for rule breaking.

5. When confronted with a conflict among your students, you will first need to

A. immediately call in all parents/guardians of involved students.

B. refrain from any accusations and gather information about what happened.

C. state that none of the participants may speak at this time.

D. refrain from bringing in any other witnesses.

Answers

1. **B**

2. **A**

3. **B**

4. **B**

5. **B**

Competency 5

Understand strategies for creating an organized
and productive learning environment and for
promoting students' ability to monitor their
own behavior

Strategies for Organization and Student Self-Monitoring of Behavior

When considering how to implement effective classroom routines and procedures, it is important to note the following:

- Students thrive on having predictable routines.

- Students are much more distracted when routines are changed or interrupted.

- It is important to stay on a regular schedule and keep with the same routine every day, but that is not always possible. The daily routine can often be interrupted.

- Having a plan for routine and procedure (whether it is followed or not) at least gives the students structure.

A positive learning environment is based on good classroom management. The environment is most productive when effective routines and procedures are developed and then followed by students and teachers. By having routines and procedures, it is easier for students to cope with the changes and distractions that will occur throughout the school year.

After a major (or even a minor) disruption to the daily schedule, like a pep rally or fire drill, when the students return to their normal schedule, even if it is modified, they will be more prepared and willing to get back to the process of learning when they have expectations of routines and procedures that are established and consistently used.

When developing routines and procedures for use in the learning environment, the teacher should consider the following:

1. Routines and procedures must be appropriate and applicable to the students. Students at different levels of development have vastly different needs for routines and procedures. For example, a high school student does not need to be taught routines and procedures like lining up and changing classes, the way an elementary-school student would need to be taught.

2. The teacher should decide which routines and procedures are the most important to use in the learning environment. Not every task needs them, but most tasks can benefit from them. For example, students can be taught to read an AR (Accelerated Reader) book when finished with assignments so they will not need to ask what to do next or get into trouble. Students can also be taught how to turn in assignments with a name and student number on top of each assignment and then put that work into the proper class folder or assignment box.

3. The teacher must decide how routines and procedures can enhance the learning environment. In the previous example of having students read AR books when finished with assignments, other students can continue working without distractions. The teacher can both monitor the class and work with individuals without having to spend time finding additional work to keep students busy, plus dealing with behavior disruptions. Teachers can design routines and procedures with the interests of both themselves and their students in mind, resulting in an enhanced learning environment for everyone.

4. Too many procedures can overwhelm students. A procedure is not needed for everything that is done. Students can usually figure out the correct thing to do when there is not a procedure in place for it. Too many procedures can also be difficult to remember. If there are a large number of procedures, it is better to introduce several each day rather than all of them at one time or in the same day.

Following is the first of four skills described in this chapter that are needed for mastery of Competency 5:

> *Demonstrate knowledge of how to manage the instructional environment to optimize time on task for students at different developmental levels (e.g., organizing a daily schedule, managing transitions, managing materials, handling unanticipated situations).*

The teacher must manage an instructional environment for students at different developmental levels. In today's educational climate, the classroom contains students of varying ability levels. In the previous section, an example was used to demonstrate how students could be taught to read AR books when finished with assignments so that they would not need to ask what to do after completion.

In the differentiated learning environments of today, it is not enough to give everyone the same assignment, wait for everyone to finish, and then continue with the next task, activity, or assignment. With the variety of ability levels in each classroom, a teacher has to plan for different students doing different assignments. Assignments must be planned and organized to ensure that they help students learn the information being taught, as well as meet the standards; assignments must also be practical so that they can be completed by the students for whom they were assigned and can be completed within a planned amount of time. The ultimate goal of the differentiated classroom is to achieve maximum personal growth and individual success.

To get the best results for all students in the differentiated learning environment, the teacher must manage the instructional content and optimize time on tasks for each student. Many students have similar ability levels, so there is no need to have a separate and unique assignment for each student in the class; however, each student's unique needs, abilities, and interests should always be taken into account when planning tasks for the students in differentiated learning environments. Being flexible is the key to planning tasks for students, as well as being ready to make changes to planned instruction. There will always be unanticipated situations to deal with each day, and how these situations are managed will determine the effectiveness of instruction.

GACE Tip

The key to planning instruction is flexibility.

Several principles of differentiated instruction can help the teacher plan instruction, including the following:

1. Assessment is an ongoing process. The assessment of students and their progress influences the upcoming instruction.

2. Many different instructional strategies are used in the learning environment. These, of course, are based on the individual learning needs of the students.

3. Multiple types of resources are used. Some students may use different resources from those of other students in the same class. The use of different materials may be based on abilities or on the differentiated instruction itself.

4. Problem solving is done by students. In traditional classrooms, teachers are the primary problem solvers, and students learn problem-solving techniques from the teacher. Students learn more from doing the work on their own than from watching and learning as the teacher does the work.

5. The student and teacher can collaborate. Instruction and tasks are based on the needs of the student. The teacher and student collaborate to determine the best and most meaningful methods of instruction for the student in the differentiated learning environment.

6. The ultimate goal of the differentiated classroom is to achieve maximum personal growth and individual success. Assessment is done on an individual basis. Instruction is tailored to the needs of the individual, and the student has some input into the instruction by collaborating with the teacher to decide on instruction and assessment.

> *Analyze the effects of classroom management strategies on attitudes and behavior and on the attainment of student learning goals.*

The differentiated learning environment is a collaboration between students and teachers. That collaboration depends on—and is influenced by—classroom management strategies. Because students have a stake in their instruction when collaborating with the teacher, they also have a responsibility to the teacher for their behavior.

A student is always held responsible for his own behavior, but in a differentiated learning environment where the student has some control of his own instruction when collaborating with the teacher, the teacher can require even more responsibility and more severe consequences for behavior that does not fit classroom procedures. Students with behavior modifications who are placed in a differentiated learning environment collaborate with the teacher to set goals; the student and teacher collaborate to find a way for the student to meet his learning goals and follow the procedures of the class; the teacher and student agree on these goals.

Ultimately, however, the teacher is responsible for the learning environment. The teacher must use effective classroom-management strategies to set goals for student behavior and student learning.

Following are tips that teachers can use to improve their classroom management skills:

1. Plan and manage instructional techniques prior to teaching.

2. Use instructional time effectively.

3. Help students develop a sense of fairness and respect.

4. Establish and maintain rapport with students.

5. Communicate and demonstrate appropriate behavioral standards.

6. Search for techniques to improve the learning environment.

> *Demonstrate knowledge of strategies for promoting students' ability to collaborate and work productively during cooperative-learning and small-group activities.*

Many schools use the learning-focused method for student learning. This method relies heavily on collaboration among students working in small groups, working in pairs, and many other collaborative groups for students.

Schools and learning environments that use methods other than learning-focused methods use these very same methods for collaboration among students. There are all forms of cooperative learning, and their main goal is to get students to be more involved, work more productively with others, and help teach each other by assessing each other's knowledge.

Some elements of cooperative learning are as follows:

1. **Positive interdependence.** Students rely on the knowledge they receive from each other. Each student has a responsibility to put forth effort, or the other group members suffer.

2. **Face-to-face interaction.** Students learn to work in a group with other members face-to-face.

3. **Individual accountability.** Each student must contribute and be a viable member of the team.

4. **Social skills.** Students build social skills through group interactions.

5. **Group processing.** Many different points of view are given. A group must work together and agree on ways to solve problems and complete assignments.

Collaborative and cooperative groups and pairs can take many forms. They may be used to accomplish tasks and complete assignments in many different ways, including the following:

1. **Pair share.** Place students in pairs. One member of the pair will be required to answer a question or tell a fact to the other. The same or a similar requirement will be given to the other student. This can be an ongoing pairing so that the teacher can tell the class members to get with their partner. From this pairing, the teacher can lead other activities or accomplish other tasks.

2. **Three-step interview.** Use this as an icebreaker, or assign roles to students who then discuss various topics. To start, every student pairs up with one other student. One of the pair interviews the other by asking probing and thoughtful questions. After the desired number of minutes, they switch roles and the other student interviews. An example of the process is this: as a student interviews, she writes her answers down; she then pairs up with someone new. First, she tells the new person what she learned in the first interview; then she goes through the interview process with the new partner. This can continue as many times as desired.

3. **Structured problem solving.** Place students in small groups. Give each group a task, ask them to brainstorm, or give them a problem to solve. The group should complete the task, and all members should be prepared to give an answer or response to the class. Each member of the group will be given a different number. A number will be chosen, and that member of the group will give the response or answer to the class.

4. **Focused listing.** Use focused listening as a brainstorming technique or as a technique to generate descriptions and definitions for concepts. Students then generate words to define or describe something; the list is then used to start group or class activities. Small groups can compare lists of words for different topics and choose the word or words that best fit the topic.

5. **Paired annotations.** Pair students up. Ask them to complete the same task, such as reading a chapter and answering the review questions. After completing the task individually, the pairs of students compare their answers and look for differences; they then find out whether one is incorrect.

6. **Jigsaw.** Start students in small groups, and assign each group a topic. Every member of the group becomes an "expert" for the assigned topic. The next step is to rearrange groups so there is one expert for each topic in each of the new groups. The experts in each group then take turns teaching everyone in their new group the information from their first topic.

7. **Round-robin brainstorming.** Divide the class into small groups. Assign one student to be the recorder. Give the class a question that has many different answers; give them a few moments to think of some answers. Members of the group give answers, and the recorder writes them all down. The teacher then leads a class discussion of the various answers from the groups.

8. **Three-minute review.** Stop at any time during a lecture, activity, or task. Give small groups three minutes to summarize the material, review what was said, or answer questions.

9. **Send a problem.** Place students in small groups. Each student creates a card with a question on one side and the answer on the other side. Each member reads the question to the group; if all members agree on the answer, they pass the question-and-answer card to the next group. The next group takes the cards from another group; they read the questions and answer them. If they all agree on the answer, they continue to pass the question-and-answer card to the next group.

10. **Team expectations.** This is a method for determining expectations of members of a group to perform a task in a group setting. Place students in small groups and ask them to create a form that lists behaviors that are expected of individuals, pairs, and the group as a whole. The result can then be used for all group tasks and activities.

11. **Uncommon commonalities.** Place students in small groups. Four students work well for this activity. Each student writes down a list of things about the topic; discuss all members' items. Then, they make a list of the topics proposed by all four members, three members, and so on. This can be used for members to list things about themselves—an exercise in getting acquainted.

12. **Guided reciprocal pair questioning.** Place students in small groups. Students then use information from lectures, readings, videos, or other sources to write questions based on the material. Students do not have to be able to answer the questions they write. In groups, they can read the questions and discuss possible answers; then continue with another question.

13. **Group investigations.** Place students in small groups, which then choose or are assigned a topic. The students in the group work together to create a group project or complete a task. This is a cooperative group that will use higher-order thinking skills and could be used to complete major projects on different topics.

14. **Write around.** Place students in small groups—a technique that is often used for creative writing. Each student begins a story or other writing with a single sentence, then passes the paper to the right. The next student adds a sentence to the paper and passes the paper to the right again. This can continue for as long as necessary.

Before collaboration and cooperation within groups can begin, the teacher must take steps to prepare for the tasks:

1. Decide what content should be taught and how it will be assessed. The teacher should determine whether the activity will be part of a larger lesson or the sole basis for instruction of the material.

2. Determine the most useful cooperative-learning technique from the list. Then choose which groups or pairs the students need to be divided into.

3. Choose a setup for the learning environment that will be the most useful for the chosen groups and cooperative-learning method.

4. The teacher communicates the expectations for the activity, including all steps to the process and the amount of time allowed for the activity. It may be necessary to divide the activity into different parts or stages, depending on the material covered, the cooperative-learning method used, and the amount of time needed to complete and master all content that is assessed.

5. The teacher should provide any instruction and model all necessary parts of the activity to ensure complete understanding of the expectations for the students. Students should clearly understand the expectations and how the activity will be assessed.

6. The teacher should monitor students as they work on and complete the activity to see that they are following directions and completing all parts of the activity properly.

7. Depending on the method for assessment, some students may be required or asked to demonstrate what was learned as part of the activity.

8. The teacher should evaluate effort by groups and provide feedback to encourage students and reward superior work. Students not meeting the standards for assessment should conference with the teacher privately at an appropriate time.

> *Recognize effective methods for encouraging students to monitor their own behavior and for promoting students' sense of responsibility and accountability in the classroom (e.g., communicating developmentally appropriate behavior expectations, involving students in developing positive rules and procedures, establishing and consistently enforcing clear consequences for behavior, valuing academic integrity).*

Discipline is a necessary element of the learning environment. The teacher sets the rules and procedures that must be followed in the classroom. The rules and procedures must always be clearly understood by students, and the consequences for breaking the rules must be fair and consistent for all students in all situations. This method has worked well in education for a very long time. Recently, there has been much discussion about trying to get students to take responsibility for their own behavior and learning. Many students have never had to take responsibility for their behavior or actions, so this can be difficult for many of them. Not having taken responsibility for their own behavior and learning has resulted in many of the behavior problems and lack of motivation seen in many students today. Ideally, getting students to monitor their own behavior and learning would result in better students all around.

Here are some steps for implementing a behavior self-management system in the learning environment:

1. Choose one behavior to begin focusing on.

2. When that first behavior begins to reach an acceptable level, introduce a second behavior into the student's self-management system.

3. Define for the student the exact behavior to be monitored. Be sure the student is clear on the expectations and understands how to monitor his or her own behavior.

4. Decide how and where the student is to keep track of his or her own behavior.

5. Set a period of time for the student to begin monitoring the behavior.

6. Check the student's accuracy on a regular basis. When the student has demonstrated accuracy, check for it randomly.

7. Give the student many chances for self-monitoring. Provide positive feedback. Reward the student for correcting his or her behavior through self-monitoring.

Sample Questions for Competency 5

1. A positive learning environment is

   A. created by strict discipline.

   B. created by making friends with the students.

C.   most productive when effective routines and procedures are developed and then followed by students and teachers.

D.   created by not interacting with the students in a friendly manner until midterm.

2.   Routines and procedures in the classroom need to be determined by

A.   the developmental level of the students.

B.   the needs of the teacher for directed focus in the classroom.

C.   the number of students in the classroom.

D.   the diversity of the students in the classroom.

3.   The number of classroom rules

A.   should be as many as can be thought of to respond to every conceivable situation.

B.   should be few enough to be remembered by the students.

C.   should cover every situation that the teacher has encountered in his or her career.

D.   are immaterial to classroom behavior.

4.   The following are important when using differentiated instruction EXCEPT

A.   Assessment needs to be ongoing.

B.   Many strategies need to be used.

C.   The teacher needs to control all problem-solving situations.

D.   The ultimate goal is personal growth and individual success.

5.   Behavior management needs to start with

A.   consequences for misbehavior.

B.   a strict, firm demeanor when dealing with the child.

C.   a way of keeping score.

D.   one behavior at a time.

Answers

1. **C**

2. **A**

3. **B**

4. **C**

5. **D**

Competency 6

6

Understand principles and practices of effective motivation and communication in the classroom and how to apply this knowledge to promote student learning and encourage active engagement in the learning process

Principles and Practices of Effective Communication in the Classroom

Intrinsic and extrinsic motivation are both used in the learning environment. We have all known or heard of parents who try to motivate their child by rewarding him or her for good grades. This is a form of extrinsic motivation. Intrinsic motivation, on the other hand, is self-motivation. Self-motivated students work hard for their own satisfaction because they want to do well, not because someone else is rewarding them or forcing them to do something. Students who are intrinsically motivated are much preferred to those who are extrinsically motivated. Students who are only motivated extrinsically will do exactly what is needed (and nothing more) to receive the reward, or they will complete the minimum amount of work required so they can move on to the next level. For example, an extrinsically motivated student who has been told that she will receive $50 if she makes A/B honor roll will put out just enough effort to make the required B in each class.

Students do not challenge themselves often, and parents do not usually set goals that cannot be reached or that require too much effort on the part of the student.

Within the learning environment, the teacher will have students who are motivated in many different ways. The intrinsically motivated students are easiest to spot. They are ready at the beginning of class, pay attention, ask questions about requirements for assignments, do quality work, and rarely engage in disruptive behavior. The students who have been extrinsically motivated by their parents to receive a reward for getting certain grades can also be spotted easily. They are normally less organized; they pay attention when the teacher talks about topics that have a bearing on their reward and ask questions about how assignments are graded and how many points questions are worth. They complete the minimum amount of work to receive a predetermined grade for each assignment, ask for extra credit, and then are more concerned with doing that than with doing well on all assignments and tests; they are usually very social in the classroom whenever they have a chance.

Each type of motivation gives the teacher tools to use in motivating students. Each method, intrinsic and extrinsic, has advantages and disadvantages for the students and the teacher. Here are some strategies for employing intrinsic and extrinsic motivation for students:

1. Use extrinsic motivation (rewards) only when a specific task is accomplished. Rewards should be given only for doing high-quality work, not doing just enough to earn the reward.

2. Use rewards sparingly. Rewards should be given in special circumstances. Students should not do work just to get a reward.

3. Give rewards as surprises. Do not tell the students that they will receive a reward for completing a task; when students are finished, reward those who completed the task correctly. This will encourage students to always do quality work and finish assignments if they think they may receive a reward.

4 Student work should always be evaluated on an individual basis and compared to the standards and requirements for the task. Work should never be compared to that of other students.

5. Answer questions from all students fairly. Some students will have different motivations for doing work and may ask questions that do not seem important. This especially includes questions about requirements for assignments, grading, and extra credit.

6. Recognize student differences. Developmental differences are also important to recognize. Encourage all students to work to the best of their ability. This will be more evident and important in a differentiated learning environment.

7. Help students to recognize personal meaning and value in all tasks. Demonstrating real-world connections can encourage students when they see the value and practical uses for the tasks they are engaged in within the learning environment.

Following is the first of seven skills required for mastery of Competency 6:

Analyze the expected outcomes of using various motivational strategies in given situations to promote learning.

When motivational strategies are used in the learning environment, several outcomes can be expected. The students who are motivated have similar characteristics. They meet common expectations because of their motivation, whether it is intrinsic or extrinsic. Some possible outcomes are as follows:

1. Students become more successful independent learners.

2. Students have success outside of academics as well.

3. Students set, meet, and exceed their goals.

4. Students are successful within the learning environment and outside the learning environment.

5. Students seek out more opportunities for learning.

6. Students have better and more expressive language skills.

7. Students expect to succeed and are confident in their abilities.

Recognize strategies for communicating high expectations to all students and for sustaining student interest in learning.

Teachers must effectively communicate high expectations to their students and should also communicate these expectations to parents. By doing so, the students, parents, and teachers are all aware of the same expectations; this helps motivate some students. Having high expectations from teachers also helps students develop more interest in learning. Expectations are presented through evaluating, communicating, and demonstrating in the learning environment. Many strategies can be used to communicate high expectations from teachers, including the following:

1. Make learning contracts with students. A learning contract is a written agreement that explains the teacher's expectations of the student. The student can see all expectations written down. Sometimes, contracts are created with student input, which strengthens student buy-in.

2. Use scoring rubrics to communicate high expectations. Students can see what is required to meet high expectations. The student is also aware of scoring for all aspects of the task with the use of a scoring rubric.

3. Use the syllabus and other written materials to communicate high expectations. When giving out materials in class, expectations can be communicated to students. Verbal instructions can be given with the written materials. The written materials can also contain the expectations from the teacher.

4. Note that the standards convey high expectations. By design, they require students to meet expectations set by the state, school system, school, and teacher. It is up to the teacher to relay these requirements to the students and explain their significance.

5. Use real-world examples to communicate high expectations. The teacher may choose to relate tasks and standards to real-world examples to emphasize their importance.

6. Communicate high expectations by being motivated, enthusiastic, caring, and supportive toward the tasks that students are required to complete. When a teacher is excited about a task, it demonstrates to the students that expectations are high for their success.

7. Communicate high expectations by reviewing students' work. Students who know that their finished work will be seen by others make more effort to meet higher expectations. Work that is displayed in the learning environment or in another location in the school can influence students, and when students post work to the Internet, do oral presentations for the class, or even exchange work with a fellow student, there is motivation to meet or even exceed the expectations of the task.

8. Provide feedback and assessment quickly and with positive responses; this communicates high expectations. When students are assessed and provided timely feedback by the teacher, they realize that the tasks are important and valued by the teacher. This demonstrates high expectations for all assignments and tasks.

> *Demonstrate knowledge of strategies for promoting students' intrinsic motivation and their sense of ownership and responsibility for their own learning (e.g., providing opportunities for self-directed learning, connecting learning to students' lives and needs, facilitating students' goal setting, providing authentic learning experiences).*

Intrinsically motivated students take a lot of responsibility on themselves. They are self-motivated; they work on projects and assignments without constant supervision and external motivation, and are satisfied by completing tasks on their own. These students take ownership and are responsible for their own learning. Sometimes, these students complete tasks or assignments without carefully following directions because they take so much responsibility for their own learning. Although these students are highly motivated

GACE Tip

Even highly motivated students have special needs.

and usually highly intelligent, they are still in need of direction by the teacher in most cases. Many students get far ahead of the lesson and miss key points because they are not paying close attention. This group of students has special needs. Because they are so highly motivated, they must be challenged to stay interested and participate in tasks and lessons.

Several techniques can be used with highly motivated students. Goals must be set so that they have goals that challenge them and give them specific tasks to work toward. Opportunities for self-directed study should also be available to these students. Because they are self-motivated, the students work very well on tasks and assignments that they can complete without constant supervision. Tasks can be agreed upon by the student and teacher; then the student can be given the resources and time to complete the assignment.

Another technique for intrinsically motivated students would be to provide authentic learning experiences. The self-motivated students would much rather complete tasks and projects than answer questions. They should be allowed, even encouraged, to complete tasks that require their direct involvement and help motivate them. By completing authentic tasks and self-directed learning, students are connected to their motivational needs and skills. These students have special skills that must be encouraged.

> *Demonstrate knowledge of how various student characteristics (e.g., age, gender, cultural background, linguistic background, exceptionality) may affect communication in the classroom.*

Teachers must be aware of student characteristics that may affect communication in the learning environment. Teachers have many types of students in each class, and each student has characteristics that may affect communication in the learning environment, resulting in either the teacher or the student having difficulty understanding the other.

1. A student's age can have an effect on communication. Students who are very young may not have completely developed vocal chords and may be difficult

to understand. Some teachers may begin to have difficulty hearing as they become older, which can affect communication with students.

2. Gender may also play a role in affecting communication between students and the teacher. Some students may find it difficult to work with and communicate with a teacher of a different gender. For example, a female student may not communicate well with male teachers because she does not have a father at home and has had no practice communicating with males in positions of authority.

3. A student's cultural background can greatly affect communication. Students may have religious or cultural beliefs that are barriers to their learning. Anything that inhibits a student's ability to learn affects communication in the learning environment.

4. Linguistics has one of the most profound effects on communications. Students who use English as their second language will always have some difficulty with the language. Even students who speak, read, and write English very well may have minor difficulties with meanings at times. Students who speak, read, and write little or no English have greater difficulty with communication in the learning environment. Students with the most severe linguistic limitations affect communication for both the student and the teacher. If the student does not understand the teacher, chances are the teacher doesn't understand the student.

5. Students with exceptionalities may have difficulty communicating in the learning environment, but in many cases adjustments can be made that greatly improve communication. For example, a student with hearing problems might wear a hearing aid, or an aide might interpret what the teacher is saying or use sign language to help the student. Because exceptionalities have usually been part of the student's life since beginning school, adjustments have been used and refined many times to make communication easier for the teacher and student in the learning environment.

> *Recognize how to communicate effectively with all students (e.g., using active listening skills, appropriate vocabulary, and nonverbal indicators) to achieve specified goals (e.g., setting expectations, providing feedback, building student self-esteem, modeling appropriate communication).*

Teachers must communicate effectively with all students to ensure learning. It is only when all communication is understood that students will receive the most benefit from the task or lesson that the teacher is communicating to the students. The teacher must use active listening skills to get feedback from students; that is, teachers ask questions of students, and students give answers and also ask questions of their own. It is up to the teacher to use active listening skills to ensure effective communication between the student and teacher.

Teachers must also use appropriate vocabulary when communicating with students, which means using proper English when speaking, reading, and writing to model how effective communication is used. Appropriate vocabulary also includes using vocabulary and terminology that is appropriate, consistent, and effective for the course of study in the learning environment. For example, geometry terms must be used correctly in all levels of education so negative meanings for vocabulary terms are never used, even at a very young age. Sometimes, teachers deliberately use terms that make sense to younger students but may be incorrect so that younger students can understand a concept. Later, the students might be told that the term was used incorrectly before, but now that they are in a higher-level course, they are to use the term correctly. Using the term incorrectly at a younger age, even if it is a deliberate misuse by the teacher, reinforces negative meanings and can lead to confusion later.

Teachers may also use nonverbal indicators to communicate with students. Body language, hand gestures, and facial expressions are all forms of nonverbal indicators used by everyone. Although teachers may choose to use these indicators, they must be very careful; some indicators can be misunderstood, or students may completely miss them, either because they do not understand the meaning or they are not paying attention.

Effective communication between students and teachers is important for setting expectations, providing feedback, building student self-esteem, and modeling appropriate communication. Expectations between teachers and students are essential if students are to understand what the

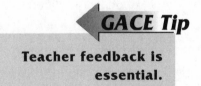

GACE Tip

Teacher feedback is essential.

teacher expects. The teacher must effectively communicate this to the students. When there is a misunderstanding, students may end up doing things incorrectly, spending a lot of time working on the wrong assignment or task, or not completing essential tasks. Feedback is necessary for a student to understand what a teacher thinks about an assignment, what grade is given for an assignment, or how the student can improve on an assignment.

Student self-esteem is closely tied to effective communication by a teacher. With many students in a class, the teacher must effectively communicate praise to each student. This will contribute to the self-esteem of the student and is necessary for student growth.

For some students, praise does not come very often, so it is important to communicate positive feedback effectively. Finally, teachers must model effective communication. Students watch and listen to everything the teacher does. When the teacher does not communicate effectively, students see this and do not try to communicate effectively and properly themselves.

> *Demonstrate knowledge of strategies for adjusting communication to promote student understanding and engagement.*

Teachers must adjust communication to promote student understanding and engagement. Students cannot and will not learn if they are not engaged in the lesson and do not understand the lesson. Effective communication promotes student understanding. Teachers must adjust techniques and styles to meet the requirements of their students. Students, even from class-to-class, learn in different ways. To promote understanding, a teacher must be aware of these differences and be willing to make changes to accommodate the differences. Teachers must use effective questioning to check for student understanding and then make changes to their strategies for communication to reach the learning objectives for the students.

Students must also be engaged by the material and the teacher so that they will be interested enough to learn the required objectives. Students who are not engaged will not learn from the teacher, no matter what they do; students who are engaged are best prepared for and open to learning. Teachers must use effective communication to get students' attention and hold that attention throughout the lecture, demonstration, or task. Motivation is a key factor in getting a student engaged. Many techniques for motivating students were discussed earlier in this chapter. Using these techniques, along with effective communication and techniques for effective questioning, will help to engage students and keep them engaged throughout the learning process.

> *Demonstrate knowledge of different purposes for questioning (e.g., promoting recall, evaluating student understanding, promoting higher-order thinking), and applying techniques for effective questioning in varied learning contexts.*

Questioning is a very useful technique for teachers and has many purposes. The Socratic method of questioning requires that students use critical-thinking skills to try to answer questions, which is different from giving direct answers to direct questions. Both the direct question-and-answer and the Socratic method have their use in the learning environment. Some of these are as follows:

1. Finding out what the student already knows is one of the most common and widely used purposes of questioning. The teacher asks questions that students can answer from material they have been working with in the learning environment.

2. Promoting a discussion is another purpose of questioning. The teacher asks students to offer opinions or share experiences in order to generate participation in a topic.

3. Checking for understanding is used to find out what the student knows or understands. For example, the teacher may ask for an answer to a problem or a review question. It may also be used to confirm that students are sure of what they have been told. For example, a teacher could ask students what they are supposed to do when they are finished with their assignments, and the students would respond by telling the teacher they are to be quiet and read their library books.

4. Questions can be used when students disrupt class. The teacher could ask a student who is talking if it is all right to continue teaching class or should everyone stop and wait for the student to finish talking or displaying the disruptive behavior. The question is directed to the student and includes a question about his or her behavior.

5. Another purpose of questioning is to gather information about the student. A teacher may ask a student what he did during the weekend or ask what kinds of sports he enjoys playing. This type of questioning may not directly relate to the class materials and student learning but does build a better relationship between the teacher and student.

6. Motivating students is another purpose of questioning. Questions may be asked to get the students interested in a topic and motivate them to pay attention and participate in the learning environment. For example, a teacher may ask the class if they know how mummies were made.

7. Another purpose of questioning is for reflection. Getting students to reflect on what they have learned or read is a good skill to develop, and a teacher can prompt students to do this by questioning them.

8. Questioning can be used to reinforce learning. Students may be asked questions that require them to review or summarize learning that has recently taken place.

9. Questions can give listeners a break from a presentation. After a teacher has been lecturing or presenting material in some way, questions may be asked to give students a break from listening, be a transition between topics, or offer students a chance to participate in the presentation.

10. Directing student thinking is another purpose for questioning. A student may be asked what steps are needed to solve a problem. The question would be directly about the topic the teacher is trying to teach and would be posed to help the student recall and use information to solve a problem or perform a task.

Effective questioning by teachers is a critical skill that benefits students in the learning environment. Questions have many purposes that promote higher-order thinking skills, recall, and assessment for students. The purposes of questions will not be met, however, unless the questions are effective. A teacher must use questions correctly to illicit the desired response from the student. Using effective questioning techniques is imperative to get correct and proper responses. Here are some techniques for effective questioning:

1. Create a safe learning environment for asking and answering questions. Students will not answer questions if they are afraid of consequences for getting their answers wrong. For example, if the rest of the class laughs at a student who is genuinely trying to answer a question correctly, then those students and others will not try to answer questions for fear of being laughed at.

2. Use questions that are planned for the class, and be prepared to use questions that come up during the lesson. The teacher should have questions planned and prepared but be flexible and seize opportunities to ask questions that arise during questioning, reviewing, or lecturing.

3. Use open-ended and closed-ended questions for different purposes when they are necessary. Open-ended questions do not have limits. Answers can have a very wide range and usually have no limits, or at least very large limits. Closed-ended questions are limited to a specific number of answers. Math equations would be examples of closed-ended questions.

4. After asking a question, wait patiently for an answer. Silence may be necessary. By being patient with students, they will see that the teacher is willing to wait for an answer to a question before revealing an answer or moving on to the next question or topic. Students will think about the answer to a question that they know must be answered by someone. If a teacher is not patient and answers questions if students do not, then students will simply not answer the questions and wait patiently for the teacher to do the work and answer all the questions.

5. Ask students if a given answer is correct. Do not tell the class or students right away whether the answer given was correct or incorrect. Whenever a question is answered by anyone—teacher or student—the class or an individual should be asked if the correct answer was given or asked if they agree with the answer. Several students may be asked. This can become an opportunity for a discussion when students do not agree on an answer.

6. Ask only one question at a time. This will keep students from becoming confused, keep the students thinking about the question at hand, and give the teacher an opportunity to follow up with additional questions that may arise after or during the current single question.

7. Make sure all students have an opportunity to answer questions. Do not allow just a few students to answer most of the questions. Many students must also be motivated to answer or attempt to answer questions. Take answers to questions from volunteers and nonvolunteers.

8. Carefully phrase questions. Questions should be asked in such a way to get the desired response from the students. The questions must be clear and understood by the students in order to give an answer.

9. Give feedback to answers given by the students. Probing questions can be asked in response to an answer that implies the correct answer without elaborating on it. Ask the student to elaborate. Ask further questions that require elaboration; give feedback to each response. Use hand gestures to give feedback and encourage the student to continue answering. Use silence when necessary to show the student you are waiting for more of an answer.

Sample Questions for Competency 6

1. An effective teacher can use which of the following to communicate expectations to students?

   A. Tell the students what you expect them to do.

   B. Use a rubric.

   C. It isn't necessary to communicate expectations to students.
   They should know what you expect.

   D. Display graded student work around the classroom.

2. Which of the following is NOT an example of extrinsic motivation that can be used in a classroom?

   A. Offering added points to a test for answering a bonus question.

   B. Giving students homework-free passes for good performance
   on a test.

   C. Giving praise for a good performance.

   D. Expecting students to read a particular book because you
   explain to them how good it made you feel to read this book.

3. How should teachers use rewards for good performance with students?

    A. They should be used sparingly.

    B. They should be used frequently.

    C. They should never be used.

    D. They should be used only with very bright students.

4. The use of immediate positive feedback with students produces which results?

    A. Students' self-esteem improves.

    B. Students answer more questions.

    C. Students perform better in cooperative-learning situations.

    D. Students stay on task better.

5. Why is it important for teachers to determine students' prior knowledge before beginning a new topic?

    A. It allows prior knowledge to be incorporated in the teaching strategy as a bridge to understanding the new material.

    B. It gives a definitive starting point for the new material.

    C. It helps keep the new information organized.

    D. It allows the teacher to cover more content.

Answers

1. **B**

2. **D**

3. **A**

4. **D**

5. **A**

CHAPTER
7

Competency 7

Understand types of assessment; the relationships among goals, assessment, instruction, and learning; and how to apply various assessment strategies to support standards-based instruction

Assessments, Goals, and Assessment Strategies for Standards-Based Instruction

Assessment is extremely important in the field of education. Because there are national and state standards, standardized testing, and other testing requirements, many people look toward tests as the final measurement of student achievement. Educators must know the characteristics that mark formal and informal assessments.

A *formal assessment* is defined as an assessment that generates data that support the conclusions drawn from the test. Educators usually refer to these types of assessments as standardized measures. These tests have been tried on students previously and have generated statistics that support a particular conclusion—for example, that the student is reading "below average" for his age. The data on formal assessments are mathematically computed and summarized. Scores such as percentiles or standard scores most commonly result from this type of assessment.

It is believed, however, that a wide variety of assessment tools should be incorporated in order to evaluate all aspects of the education that students receive. This is why both formal and informal assessment, rubrics, and performance-based assessments should be used in teaching. An *informal assessment* is best defined as an assessment that *is not*

GACE Tip

Use informal assessments to guide your instruction.

data-driven but is content- and performance-driven. For example, running records are informal assessments because they indicate how well a student is reading a specific book. Scores for this type of assessment might be, for example, 10 correct out of 15, percentage of words read correctly. In any case, the assessment should match the purpose of assessing. Formal or standardized measures should be used to assess overall achievement, to compare a student's performance with others at the student's age or grade, or to identify comparable strengths and weaknesses with peers. Informal assessments, which are sometimes referred to as criterion-referenced measures or performance-based measures, should be used to inform instruction.

As stated earlier, there are many ways to assess student achievement. Most commonly used are the criterion-referenced test, norm-referenced test, teacher-made test, performance-based assessment, portfolio, teacher observation, peer assessment, and student self-assessment. Teachers must know how to use the fundamental standardized tests and interpret them (for validity and reliability), construct formal assessments, use informal assessments, and use assessment information for the purposes of grading. Key points to remember when comparing limitations, characteristics, and advantages of aforementioned assessments and tests are as follows.

Standardized assessments may be norm-referenced or criterion-referenced.

1. *Criterion-referenced tests* determine the specific knowledge and skills a student possesses. Thus this form of testing "uses as its interpretive frame of reference a specified content domain, rather than a specified population of persons" (Anastasi 97). Competency tests, such as the Iowa Tests of Basic Skills, represent a specific subcategory of criterion-referenced assessment and are used to ensure that students possess minimal basic skills.

2. *Norm-referenced assessments* compare individual students' scores to those of a norm-reference group, generally students of the same grade or age. They are designed to demonstrate "differences between and among students to produce a dependable rank order" (Bond 1996, 1) and are often used to classify students for ability grouping or to help identify them for placement in special programs. They are also used to provide information to report to parents.

3. *Teacher-made assessments* are constructed by an individual teacher or a group of teachers in order to measure the outcome of classroom instruction.

4. *Performance-based assessments* ask students to show what they can do when given an authentic *task,* which is then judged using a specific set of criteria.

5. *Portfolio assessment* is a process that can serve a variety of purposes. A portfolio is a collection of student work that can exhibit a student's efforts, progress, and achievements in various areas of the curriculum. A portfolio assessment can be an examination of student-selected samples of work experiences and documents related to outcomes being assessed, and it can address and support progress toward achieving academic goals, including student efficacy.

6. *Teacher observation* is a direct means for learning about students, including what they do or do not know and can or cannot do. This information makes it possible for the teacher to plan ways to encourage students' strengths and to work on their weaknesses. Observation is most effective when it follows a systematic plan. This might involve, for instance, seeing and recording which students use physical materials, which do most of the problems mentally, which use thinking strategies, and which rely on memorized facts. It may also be helpful at times to focus on observing one student within the context of a group setting.

7. *Peer assessment* is a type of assessment in which students comment on and judge their colleagues' work.

8. *Student assessment* seeks to support and improve student learning. It is the result of a movement toward accountability and involves a paradigm shift from the traditional view of what teachers provide (inputs) to a concern for what students actually learn, do, and achieve (outputs).

Educators must understand the basic terminology and concepts related to assessment, evaluation, and measurement. The concepts and definitions given here are of central importance to this understanding.

Following is the first of seven required skills for Competency 7:

> ***Demonstrate knowledge and strategies for integrating assessment and instruction, align instruction with learning goals, and use assessment to monitor student progress and guide instruction.***

Assessment results have important implications for instruction. The goal of assessment is to promote the learning of pertinent academic content for all students. School communities use assessment results in formative ways, most notably, to determine how well they are meeting instructional goals and how to alter curriculum and instruction so that goals can be better met. However, unless the content of assessment (the very thing the school assesses) and the blueprint (format) of assessment (how schools assess) match what is being taught and how it is taught, the results are meaningless. The same is true if assessment tools are not of the highest quality.

> ### *Recognize the importance of using multiple assessment strategies.*

Students are responsible for achieving high educational standards. Therefore, it is ethically necessary that educators develop and employ methods of assessment that equitably gauge and interpret student performance. Students need to be protected from unjust and academically harmful interpretations. Parents and communities deserve an accurate general picture of student achievement. Because of this, teachers need to be aware of the strengths and weaknesses in alternative assessment practices. *Differentiation* is such a method.

Differentiation is a method that enables teachers to plan strategically in order to meet the needs of the diverse learners in classrooms today, so that they may achieve targeted standards. When implemented correctly, alternative assessment is this type of instructional method. As students come to school with varying learning styles and numerous intelligences, differentiated instruction becomes a means of addressing the learning needs of everyone in the classroom. Alternative assessment also serves as a tool to assess this broad spectrum of learners. Educators know that there is not "one way" to teach students, hence the existence of differentiated instruction and alternative assessment. Today, teachers are vigorously using numerous strategies and methods to adjust the learning in his or her classroom to fit the learner instead of using the same teaching and assessing strategies for the entire population of the class. (Chapman and Gregory 2002) Assessment as ongoing feedback is a necessary component of the learning process. Assessment should not be something that comes at the end of instruction—rather, it should be ongoing throughout the lesson. The challenge for the educator is to find numerous ways to facilitate ongoing feedback for students that will increase their chances to grow and improve their learning.

> ### *Identify strategies for providing students with accurate, timely feedback.*

Feedback is a strategy that enables students to ascertain from their teachers how they are doing.

Progressive feedback challenges a student to have higher goals for a better performance overall. Sitting down with a student and offering constructive criticism, help, suggestions, and positive feedback, positively affects student learning. Marzano, Pickering, and Pollock (2001) cite providing feedback as one of the nine effective classroom strategies in their book, *Classroom Strategies that Work: Research-Based Strategies for Increasing Student Achievement.*

They tell us that effective feedback should

- be "corrective" in nature. Feedback should provide students with an explanation of what they are doing correctly and what they are doing that is *not* correct.

- be timely. Immediate feedback is necessary in order for it to be the most effective.

- be specific to a criterion. Feedback should reference a specific level of skill or knowledge and not be norm-referenced.

- allow students to provide their own feedback. Students should be able to effectively monitor their own progress through self-evaluation, based on the feedback given by the teacher.

Feedback can be informal or formal. With informal feedback, teachers can "drop by" students' desks and comment on their work. This type of feedback gives students instant suggestions so they can make immediate changes. With formal feedback, students attend a conference with the teacher in which teachers check progress toward goals, discuss progress, and work with students to set new goals. Conferences help develop self-direction and protect students from the fear of failure. When students are given feedback along the way, they are able to learn from their mistakes, make the necessary changes, and achieve at higher levels. "The best feedback appears to involve an explanation as to what is accurate and what is inaccurate in terms of student responses. In addition, asking students to keep working on a task until they succeed appears to enhance achievement (Marzano, p. 96)[1]."

Feedback is responsive communication (verbal or non-verbal) showing a reaction—"teaching" through the learner's own work. Feedback can come in many forms or even from relevant professionals outside the teaching-learning relationship. Active learning requires not only prompt but also

GACE Tip

Active learning requires feedback.

specific, challenging, catalyzing feedback. Without feedback, the learner is most likely to repeat past achievements and errors rather than create new insight, ability, and competence. The most successful learning situation will come from collaboration between teacher and learner. Helpful, healthy feedback from the teacher will elicit trust and enthusiasm from the learner. In the end, they will both learn from each other.

> *Demonstrate knowledge of appropriate strategies for modifying classroom assessments for students with various characteristics and needs (e.g., English Language Learners, students with exceptionalities).*

Section 504 of the Rehabilitation Act of 1973 protects the rights of individuals with disabilities in programs and activities that receive federal funds. Section 504 provides that, "No otherwise qualified individual with a disability in the United States . . . shall, solely by reason of her or his disability, be excluded from the participation in, be denied the benefits of, or be subjected to, discrimination under any program or activity receiving Federal financial assistance." The U.S. Department of Education enforces Section 504 in programs and activities that receive funds from the U.S. Department of Education. Recipients of these funds include public school districts, institutions of higher education, and other state and local education agencies. The Department of Education has published a regulation implementing Section 504 (34 C.F.R. Part 104) and maintains an Office for Civil Rights (OCR), with twelve enforcement offices and a headquarters office in Washington, D.C., to enforce Section 504 and other civil rights laws that pertain to recipients of funds. All students are entitled to an appropriate education, whether they have a disability or not. Services designed to meet the unique needs of children with disabilities ensure that the rights of disabled children and their parents or guardians are protected. These services also assist states and localities in providing education for all handicapped children. Furthermore, these services assess and ensure the effectiveness of efforts to educate handicapped children.

"Students with English as a second language (ESL) constitute a significant percentage of the population of our nation's schools. This population continues to increase more rapidly than that of native English-speaking students. The language-minority population has a high drop-out rate. These students are also among the lowest ranking in academic achievement and expectations. They represent an at-risk population faced with a wide range of challenges (Thompson)"[2].

In the past, students with exceptionalities were often segregated from the regular classroom. *Mainstreaming* began the process of integrating them with nondisabled students, and *inclusion* takes the process further by creating a web of services. Inclusion is most effective when regular education and special-education teachers closely collaborate on instructional adaptations for learners with exceptionalities. Federal laws and regulations require that students with exceptionalities be taught in the least restrictive environment, guarantee the right to parental involvement through due process, protect against discrimination in testing, and provide learners with full educational opportunities that include an Individual Education Program or IEP[3].

Traditionally, ESOL (English to Speakers of Other Languages) teachers have had to create original assessment tools to place low-level English language learners into their classrooms.

The following assessment strategies excerpted from *www.nwrel.org/nwreport/nov99/ materials.html* can aid in assessing ESOL students and students with disabilities:

- Focus on documenting individual student growth over time rather than comparing students with one another.

- Emphasize students' strengths (what they know) rather than weaknesses (what they don't know).

- Consider the learning styles, language proficiencies, cultural and educational backgrounds, and grade levels of students.

The following list excerpted from *www.nclrc.org/essentials/assessing/alternative.htm* depicts Alternative Assessment Guideline Strategies for disabled and ESOL students:

- Assessment is based on authentic tasks that demonstrate learners' ability to accomplish communication goals.

- Instructor and learners focus on communication, not on right and wrong answers.

- Learners help to set the criteria for successful completion of communication tasks.

- Learners have opportunities to assess themselves and their peers.

- These opportunities are built around topics or issues of interest to the students.

- They replicate real-world communication contexts and situations.

- They involve multistage tasks and real problems that require creative use of language rather than simple repetition.

- They require learners to produce a quality product or performance.

- Their evaluation criteria and standards are known to the student.

- They involve interaction between assessor (instructor, peers, self) and person assessed.

- They allow for self-evaluation and self-correction as they proceed.

> *Analyze strategies for creating and using rubrics and checklists to evaluate student performance and products.*

Rubrics allow teachers to be more objective in grading student performances. Rubrics also allow students to understand more clearly just what their teacher expects of them in each given project, assignment, or activity. Students and teachers can construct rubrics together.

Rubrics serve both student and teacher best when they are used as tools to give reference points for expectations of student work and achievement. Rubrics can improve student performance, as well as monitor it, by making teachers' expectations clear and by showing students how to meet those expectations. Rubrics are a critical and vital link between assessment and instruction. They give students the chance to be pedants, as they complete expected assignments for their teachers. The result of an implemented rubric in the classroom is usually marked improvement in the quality of student work and in learning. The most common argument for using rubrics is that they help define *quality* for both teacher and student. Rubrics help students become more thoughtful judges of the quality of their own work, as well as the work of others. When used to guide assessment, students become aware of the mistakes they made while doing their different assignments. This assessment of one's own work, moreover, increases students' sense of responsibility for the type of work they turn in, often improving the quality of that work and leaving the teacher to assess work that the student has, more often than not, already assessed.

When implementing the rubric, teachers should consider the following steps:

Step 1: Determine what skills are to be evaluated. Mechanics, format, use of a particular literary device, and spelling and organization are some common criteria. Limit yourself to three to five criteria. When more than seven are used for older students, research shows a risk for loss of student focus.

Step 2: Create a rating scale. Typically, the scale includes point values or grades A through F. However, rubrics can use performance ratings such as "Exceptional," "Successful," "Improving," or "Needs Improvement" for a more holistic approach.

Step 3: Write your criteria along the left side of a chart, and put your performance ratings along the top. Now fill in the middle of the grid with performance descriptors. For example, if your criterion is spelling and you move along the row under the column heading of performance rating C, you might fill in something like "Makes repeated spelling errors throughout essay." For a D to F grade it might read "Frequent spelling errors interfere with reader's ability to comprehend."

Step 4: Using language that is absolute can help you create your performance descriptors. It is easier to assess if you use specifics like "three or more times," or "always," or "seldom." Words and phrases like these will help you craft a better rubric.

Step 5: Review the rubric with students when you first assign the task. Answer questions they may have, and encourage them to share it with their parents.

Step 6: Check online and visit rubric-making sites to save time. Teachers can use pre-made rubrics for assignments.

> *Recognize central concepts in assessment (e.g., reliability, validity, bias) and the various purposes of assessment (e.g., monitoring, comparing, screening, diagnosing), and using this knowledge to select appropriate assessments and interpret assessment results.*

In order for assessments to be plainspoken and fair, they cannot show any forms of bias, distortion, or partiality. *Reliability* is one of two concepts used for defining and measuring bias and distortion in assessments. *Reliability* refers to the measure in which assessments are consistent and reflect on the consistency of assessment scores. For example, on a reliable test, a student would expect to achieve the same score, no matter when the student completed the assessment, when the response was scored, and who scored the response. On an unreliable examination, a student's score may vary, based on factors that are not related to the purpose of the assessment.

Another measure of reliability is the internal consistency of the items. For example, if you create a quiz to measure students' ability to solve quadratic equations, you should be able to assume that if a student gets an item correct, he or she will also get other, similar items correct. The following table outlines three common reliability measures.

Type of Reliability	How to Measure
Test-Retest	Reliability is measured by the correlation between scores of the same test given twice, at an appropriate interval.
Alternate Form	Reliability is measured by the correlation between scores of two slightly different tests.
Internal Consistency	Reliability is measured by the correlation of one part of the test to another part of the same test. Methods such as the Kuder-Richardson Formula 20 (KR20) and Cronbach's Alpha are useful in this approach.

Reliability is gauged on a scale of 0 to 1.0, 0 meaning no reliability, and 1.0 meaning perfect reliability. No test is error-free, so a score of 1.0 is impossible. A score of .80 or above on a standardized test indicates very good reliability, and a score of .50 or below indicates very poor reliability.

Validity is another standard for measuring aberrations in assessments. Validity measures accuracy—whether or not the test is assessing what it is meant to assess. Reliability and validity are independent qualities; a test may be reliable but invalid, and it may be valid but unreliable. Because of the value that students, educators, parents, and society place on assessment scores, validity is essential—more so than reliability. Also, a high validity usually indicates a high reliability.

> *Demonstrate knowledge of strategies for helping students use teacher, peer, and self-assessments to guide their own learning.*

One of the ways students ascertain quality of work is by evaluating the work of their classmates or peers. Peer assessment can be beneficial, as it can be used to involve students more closely in their learning and its evaluation. Peer assessment can also help promote an understanding in a student as to what is required of him or her. As beneficial as peer assessment is, to offer helpful feedback students must have a coherent view of what they are to look for in their peers' work. Therefore, teachers must explain expectations clearly to students before they begin peer assessment. Providing students with a practice session with a "fictional student" who completed "sample assignments" can help to introduce the mechanics of peer assessing. The teacher can provide sample writing or math work. As a group, students determine what should be assessed and how criteria for successful completion of the task should be scored. Then the instructor gives students a sample completed assignment. Students assess this using the criteria they have developed and determine how to convey feedback clearly to the fictitious student. For peer evaluation to work effectively, the learning environment in the classroom must be conducive to learning. Students must feel comfortable and trust one another in order to provide honest, unbiased, constructive feedback. Instructors who use group work and peer assessment frequently can help students develop trust by forming them into small groups early in the semester and having them work in the same groups throughout the term. This allows them to become more comfortable with each other and leads to better peer feedback.

Self-assessment can also be used to guide student learning. Self-assessment is the process of having the learners critically reflect on, record the progress of, and perhaps suggest grades for their own learning. Self-assessment may be used to help develop in students the ability to examine and think critically about their learning, to determine what criteria should be used in judging their work, and to apply these criteria objectively to their own work in order to facilitate their continuing learning.

Sample Questions for Competency 7

1. Innovations in assessment are partly a response to criticisms of the fairness and objectivity of standardized tests that have focused on all of the following EXCEPT

   A. class and gender bias.

   B. failure to measure students' general level of intelligence.

   C. failure to accurately measure students' skills.

   D. failure to measure students' levels of achievement.

2. The movement to assess student learning with ever-increasing numbers of tests has been brought on by

   A. declining test scores.

   B. international comparisons of student achievement.

   C. calls to hold teachers more accountable.

   D. all of the above.

3. When teachers measure students' attainment of knowledge and skills for the purpose of making decisions about their teaching, they are engaged in

   A. measurement.

   B. alternative assessment.

C. formative evaluation.

D. summative evaluation.

4. Most assessment approaches seek to answer the question, "Do students know content?" Performance-based assessment helps to answer what other important question?

A. Do students commit information to memory efficiently?

B. Can students reproduce what they know on tests?

C. Are students capable of creative thought?

D. How well can students use what they know?

5. Telling the story of a learner's growth in proficiency, long-term achievement, and significant accomplishments in a given academic area exemplifies the benefits of which assessment format?

A. Portfolio assessment

B. Performance-based assessment

C. Formative assessment

D. Pre-test evaluation

Answers

1. **B**

2. **D**

3. **C**

4. **D**

5. **A**

Notes

1. *www97.intel.com/en/ProjectDesign/InstructionalStrategies/Feedback/*

2. *www.finchpark.com/courses/assess/equity.htm*

3. *http://wps.prenhall.com/chet_eggen_education_6/13/3457/885175.cw/index.html*

Competency 8

Understand curricular and instructional planning procedures and how to apply effective planning to design instruction that promotes learning and achievement for all students

Curricular and Instructional Planning Procedures

Teachers in the State of Georgia plan their lessons according to the Georgia Performance Standards. Previously, Georgia teachers planned their lessons according to the Quality Core Curriculum (QCC). It was ruled in January of 2002 that the QCC objectives not only lacked depth and could not be covered in a reasonable amount of time but also did not meet national standards. The finding of the audit was that it would take 23 years—not 12—to cover the topics included at anywhere near the depth necessary for real learning to take place. Shallow standards forced teachers to guess what they should teach, without ever knowing if what they were teaching would be tested. Teachers used the curriculum not as a guide for instruction but as a reference to mention in lesson plans and then place back on the shelf.

Performance standards go into much greater depth than the content standards used in the previous curriculum. The performance standards incorporate the content standard, which simply tells the teacher what a student is expected to know (that is, what concepts he or she is expected to master) and expands on it by providing three additional items: (1) suggested tasks, (2) sample student work, and (3) teacher commentary on that work. Performance standards provide clear expectations for assessment, instruction, and student work. They define the level of work that demonstrates achievement of the standards, enabling a teacher to know "how good is good enough." The performance standards isolate and identify the skills needed to use the knowledge and skills to problem-solve, reason, communicate, and make connections with other information. Performance standards also tell the teacher how to assess the extent to which the student knows the material or can manipulate and apply the information.[1]

When constructing lesson plans, teachers must rely on an array of information to ensure that their students receive the most knowledge from each lesson. Teachers must use the Georgia Performance Standards to guide the lesson, but they must also consider students' development, characteristics, and prior experiences, students' current knowledge and skills, available time and resources, and the type of content or skills to be taught.

Writing lesson plans does not have to be difficult, but the key components mentioned earlier must be included to maximize student achievement. Here is a list of things to remember when writing lesson plans (excerpted from *http://712educators.about.com/od/lessonplans/ht/lessonplans.htm*)

1. Begin with the end in mind. What do you want the students to learn from this lesson, and what standards are you meeting? What does the State of Georgia require? What age students are you trying to reach? How are you going to assess that learning? Once you've determined this, write a quick description and list your objectives for the assignment. [This area deals with the type of content or skills to be taught.]

2. Create a key vocabulary list that you will add to as you write out your lesson plan procedure. This will help you remember terms that you need to make sure the students understand as they work through the lesson. [This area of planning deals with student development.]

3. Create a materials list and add to this as you write your procedure so that you know exactly what you will need, including A-V equipment, number of copies, page numbers from books, and so on. [This area deals with available time and resources.]

4. Determine how you will introduce the lesson. For example, will you use a simple oral explanation for the lesson, an introductory worksheet, or an interactivity of some type? [To complete this area, the teacher must consider the student's current knowledge and skill.]

5. Decide the method(s) you will use to teach the content of your lesson. For example, does it lend itself to independent reading, lecture, or whole-group discussion? Sometimes, it is best to use a combination of these methods:

beginning with a couple minutes of lecture, followed by a short whole-group discussion to ensure that the students understand what you have taught them. [To complete this area, the teacher must consider the student's current knowledge and skill.]

6. Once you have determined how you will teach the content of the lesson, write out supporting information in your notes.

7. Determine how you will have the students practice the skill or information you just taught them. For example, if you have taught them about the laws of supply-and-demand in economics, how will you have them practice this information to truly gain an understanding of the material? Will you have them complete independent practice, use a whole-group simulation, or allow students to work cooperatively on a project? These are just three possibilities for having them practice the information.

8. Once you determine how students will practice the skills that you taught them, write out step-by-step instructions.

9. Create an end-of-period review.

10. Complete details for any homework or assessments that you will be giving the students.

11. Decide on any accommodations you need to make for your class, including accommodations for ESL and special education.

12. Once you have completed your lesson plan, finish out the details, including creating the assessments, homework assignments, and any handouts.

13. Finally, make copies and collect materials for the lesson.

Following is the first of six skills required for mastering Competency 8:

Apply knowledge of how to use sources of data during planning to define learning goals, select appropriate instructional approaches and materials, and determine the sequence of instruction.

In recent years, researchers have formed a strong consensus regarding the importance of engaged learning in schools and classrooms. Teachers must know how to convey the standards to their students so they are richly engaged. There must be a clear picture for students, as they delve into what they are suppose to be learning; therefore, teachers must set learning goals for their students.

Learning goals help teachers do the following:

1. Clarify what students are to accomplish.
2. Communicate expectations to students more effectively.
3. Select methods, materials, and assignments that are most appropriate.
4. Guide assessment of what students have learned.

When constructing lesson plans, teachers must select appropriate instructional approaches (note item 3). *Instructional approaches* are strategies that determine the approach a teacher may take to achieve learning objectives. Instructional approaches can be classed as direct, indirect, interactive, experiential, or independent:

- Direct instruction, such as the lecture method, is teacher-focused.
- Indirect instruction is student-focused. Students do the cognitive work: analyzing, expressing, creating.

When your goal focuses on attitudes, values, or interpersonal outcomes, the process can have a greater importance than the product. Your focus will be on long-term retention of concepts.

Interactive instructional methods involve groups of learners. Before group work begins, it is crucial that all members know their final objectives, their time limit, and how they will be presenting their project.

Experiential instruction strategies are student-centered. The emphasis is on process, not product. These strategies are very useful for the following reasons (excerpted from *www.sasked.gov.sk.ca/docs/physed/physed6–9/instruct.html*)

- they greatly increase understanding and retention.
- students are more motivated because they actively participate and teach one another by describing what they are doing.
- they are inductive—that is, illustrations or examples are given and a rule, concept, or generalization is then formulated.
- they are activity-oriented.
- students reflect about an experience and apply what they have concluded to other contexts.

The five phases (excerpted from the same source) are as follows:

1. Experiencing (an activity occurs)

2. Sharing (reactions and observations are shared)

3. Analyzing (patterns are determined)

4. Inferring (concepts are developed)

5. Applying (plans are made to use learning in new situations)

Independent learning has implications for responsible decision making. Individuals are expected to analyze problems, consider them, make decisions, and take action. Students need to acquire lifelong learning capability. Independent learning will enable them to respond to the changing demands they will encounter in life.

When selecting appropriate instructional approaches, teachers must remember that in every class, there will be a diversity of students, each of whom will bring to the activity environment different perceptions, prior knowledge, attitudes, and learning styles. It is the teacher's responsibility to make use of an array of instructional approaches to ensure that all "types" of students and their various needs are being met.

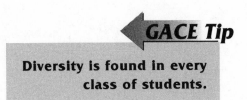

GACE Tip

Diversity is found in every class of students.

Sequence of instruction: One of the most important issues in the application of learning is sequencing of instruction. The order and organization of learning activities affects the way students process and retain information. To ensure a complete and logical sequence of instruction, there must first be a grouping of related objectives and activities. Second, there must be a sequencing of teaching activities. Objectives should be sequenced according to their learning-level hierarchy so that the instruction begins with developing knowledge and progresses to applying that knowledge after the teacher is sure that it has been understood. Learners can then be taught how to apply the knowledge and skills to a variety of situations.

Sequencing instructional events: Sequencing activities within individual lessons is necessary in order to provide a framework for teaching the content. According to Robert Gagne, there are nine events that activate processes needed for effective learning. Gagne believes all lessons should include this sequence of events.

The following list excerpted from *http://fog.ccsf.cc.ca.us/~mmalacho/OnLine/ADDIE. html* presents Gagne's nine events of instruction.

1. *Gain attention:* Start by gaining your learners' attention using an analogy, anecdote, paradox, photograph, magazine article, demonstration, or any other method. Display an outline of your lecture plan in a visual form (for example, an illustration, a summary, a diagram, a map, or chart). This gives learners a framework into which they can organize subsequent content.

2. *Inform learners of objectives:* Describe what you plan to achieve, what learners will be doing, and what they may be using. State the following: "At the end of the lecture you will be able to. . . ." Create expectancy via your objectives and description of the structure of the lecture.

3. *Stimulate recall of prior learning:* Relate your new lesson to situations or knowledge that your learners are already familiar with—for example, the previous lesson.

4. *Present stimuli with distinctive features:* Describe the key points in your lesson, emphasizing distinctive features, using a variety of techniques, if possible. For example, use photos, drawings, or some real object. Vary the format in order to maintain attention and increase comprehension.

5. *Guide learning:* Present your instruction in small steps (chunking), leading from simple to complex.

6. *Elicit performance:* Involve learners in questioning, discussing, and demonstrating to confirm what they have learned from your instruction, to increase comprehension, and to maintain attention through active participation.

7. *Provide feedback:* As learners respond to your questioning, provide them with reinforcement or remediation when necessary.

8. *Assess performance:* Use a quiz or assignment to confirm mastery of your objectives.

9. *Enhance retention and learning transfer:* Provide the opportunity for learners to apply the outcome of their training in a real-world environment—for example, realistic assignments using real data and equipment. Incorporate the full experiential learning cycle into activities so that students are encouraged to reflect on and analyze their experiences.

Recognize appropriate uses in various types of assessment information for curricular and instructional planning, including modifying lesson plans and adapting instruction to ensure all students' success in learning.

Classrooms today have students with many special needs. Teachers are often directed to "modify as necessary." The following strategies excerpted from *www.educationoasis. com/curriculum/LP/LP-resources/modifying—adapting.htm* take the mystery out of modifying and adapting materials with concrete examples and models of modifications.

If the student has difficulty becoming interested, then try

- telling stories that relate the lesson to people's lives;

- establishing relevancy and a purpose for learning by relating it to previous experiences;

- providing an experience, such as a field trip, and then teaching the lesson;

- rewarding the student often as the lesson begins;

- shaping approximations of desired behavior by providing praise, one-to-one conversation, or immediate feedback for correct answers;

- reading aloud a brief article or story to stimulate interest;

- seating the student closer to the teacher (distance affects interest); or

- making a positive, personal comment every time the student shows any evidence of interest (for example, sits in seat, has the book open).

If the student has difficulty getting started, then try

- giving a cue to begin work;

- giving work in smaller amounts;

- providing immediate feedback;

- sequencing work with easiest answers first;

- providing all necessary materials;

- introducing the assignment carefully so the student knows the task expected;

- providing time suggestions for each task;

- checking on progress often in the first few minutes of work;

- giving clear directions;

- giving a checklist for each step of the task (e.g., the steps in a long division problem); or

- using a peer or peer tutor to get the student started.

If the student has difficulty keeping track of materials or assignments, then try

- requiring a notebook or using large envelopes for each subject;
- checking his or her notebook often;
- keeping extra supplies on hand;
- giving an assignment sheet to the student, other teachers, and parents;
- writing the assignment on the board for the student to copy;
- checking and reinforcing the student for recording the assignment;
- requiring envelopes for big projects that have many separate parts;
- giving a reward (for example, grade points) for bringing a book, paper, and a pencil to class every day; or
- returning corrected work promptly.

If the student has difficulty staying on task, then try

- reducing distractions;
- increasing reinforcements;
- providing shortened tasks;
- providing checklists;
- reducing the amount of work;
- providing peer tutors;
- providing different activities during the class period;
- providing a reward valued by the student;
- isolating the student or using a time out;
- providing quiet alternatives for a short time; or
- providing a timer to set short periods of work.

If the student has trouble completing tasks on time, then try

- reducing the amount to be accomplished;
- allowing more time;

- providing time cues;

- writing schedules;

- asking for parental reinforcement;

- suggesting a calendar at home;

- providing closure at points along the way; or

- providing positive feedback to other teachers using an "assignments completed" checklist or a "wall thermometer."

If the student has trouble working in groups, then try

- providing direct instruction in group processes and providing interaction opportunities gradually;

- providing the student with a responsibility or position of leadership;

- preparing the group members to include and help the student;

- utilizing an aide or volunteer in class;

- providing more structure by defining the task and listing the steps; or

- restating the goal, linking it to the required activities, and providing closure.

If the student has trouble working independently, then try

- assigning a task at an appropriate level;

- being certain the student can see an end to the task;

- giving precise directions;

- lowering the difficulty level;

- shortening the assignment and gradually increasing the amount of work required;

- reinforcing the student for on-task behavior;

- letting the student see individual work as a sign of personal responsibility and growth rather than as a sign that the teacher just wants to "get rid of him"; or

- providing a variety of types of work within the assignment (for example, making charts, maps, or flags; drawing pictures).

> *Demonstrate knowledge of how to plan instruction that effectively integrates technology with the curriculum to support student learning.*

GACE Tip

Integrate technology across your curriculum.

Technology integration in the classroom is the inclusion of technology resources and technology-based routines into the daily work of teachers and students. Technology resources are computer hardware and specialized software, network-based communication, and other equipment. Practices include cooperative work, communication, Internet research, database management or student data tracking, and other methods to increase classroom productivity. Successful integration is difficult to define; however, it is important that integration be routine, seamless, and both efficient and effective in enhancing student learning.

Technology is ubiquitous, touching almost every part of our lives, our communities, and our homes. Properly used, technology can help students acquire the skills they need to survive in a complex, highly technological knowledge-based economy. Integrating technology into classroom instruction means more than teaching basic computer skills and software programs in a separate computer class. Effective technology integration must happen across the curriculum in ways that show a deep and enhanced learning process. In particular, four key components of learning must be supported: (1) active engagement, (2) participation in groups, (3) frequent interaction and feedback, and (4) connection to real-world experts. Effective technology integration is achieved when the use of technology is routine and transparent and when technology supports curricular goals.[2]

Research is the number-one reason to use the Internet in education. Students have a wealth of information open to them via the Internet. Often, when students research obscure topics, school libraries do not have the needed books and magazines. The Internet helps solve this problem. The possibilities for assessing research on the Internet are vast, to the benefit of both teacher and student. Some ideas include essays, debates, panel discussions, role-play, video presentation of information, Web page creation, and presentations done by Microsoft® PowerPoint®.

A second project that can help integrate technology while truly getting the students excited about school is website creation. Teachers can publish a website with their class about information the students have researched or personally created. Examples of what this page might focus on include a collection of student-created short stories, a collection of student-created poems, results and information from science fair projects, or historical letters (that is, students write as if they were historical figures)—even critiques of novels could be included. Many places offer free websites. First, teachers can check with their school to see if they have a website and whether they could create a page that would be linked to that site. If that is not available, there are many places on the Internet that can be used for the creation of such a project. In any case, student learning is clearly supported.[3]

> *Demonstrate knowledge of strategies for integrating curricula and creating interdisciplinary units of study.*

The term *integrate* means "to combine into a whole." Therefore, when developing integrated curricula, the teacher should be aiming for the students' understanding of the overall picture—how all the lessons come together and create a new and more generalized lesson—rather than the sum of the disjointed individual lessons. This is related to Gestalt theory, which holds that the whole is greater than the sum of its parts. Ideally, in an integrated curriculum, teachers and students work together to incorporate their individual personal experiences, so that the learning process is more engaging for both. When the curriculum is integrated, students are engaged and are able to draw connections among various subjects. (See *www.ncpublicschools. org/curriculum/artsed/resources/handbook/music/46introduction.*)

Interdisciplinary/cross-curricular teaching involves the simultaneous application of a theme, a problem, a principle, a process, an experience, or a value to more than one academic discipline. The organizational structure of interdisciplinary/cross-curricular teaching is built upon one theme (or unit). Upon this theme is constructed a framework of goals that specify what students will learn from the lessons that are a part of the unit. (See *www.eduplace.com/rdg/res/literacy/interd0.html.*)

Integrated curriculum is an educational principle that perceives a student's education as his or her total life experiences. Learning does not stop after the dismissal bell rings. What a child learns in school must always be focused on preparing the child to be a member of contemporary society. Theoretical subject matter is given practical applications. Traditional subject categories are replaced by broader pursuits in which cross-sections of conventional knowledge and skills come together interactively in a holistic approach to learning. The following are some strategies (excerpted from *www.todaysteacher.com/ThematicTeaching. htm*) for integrating curricula:

- A combination of subjects

- An emphasis on projects

- Sources that go beyond textbooks

- Relationships among concepts

- Thematic units as organizing principles

- Flexible schedules

- Flexible student groupings

The following are several reasons (excerpted from the same source) why integrated curriculum is important:

- Students see relationships among ideas and concepts as they plan and experience a theme-based inquiry.

- Relationships between in- and out-of-school topics become obvious to students.

- Communication processes become authentic as students engage in thematically based learning activities.

- Students are encouraged to share ideas. As they listen to one another, their personal bases of ideas are expanded.

- Respect and cooperation among peers are expanded through interaction.

- Students become more responsible for, and engaged in, their own learning.

- The teacher assumes the role of facilitator rather than information dispenser.

- A sense of community develops as cooperatively designed student activities are created.

- Many grouping patterns naturally emerge.

- Assessment is authentic, continuous, and related to learning endeavors.

> *Apply knowledge of lesson planning to evaluate a given lesson or unit plan in terms of organization, appropriateness, completeness, and feasibility.*

Teachers should analyze their lesson plans to see if they are feasible, appropriate, and complete. The first thing to consider, obviously, is what is to be taught, which should be developed based on state (or school) standards. Teachers also need to be aware of what grade level they are developing the lesson plan for and should record a time estimate for their lesson plan; this helps budget time. Once a topic is developed, teachers can begin determining how to teach the topic.

Feasibility: Teachers must ask themselves, "Is the task worthy of the time and effort required to complete it?" (The amount of time devoted to completing the task is very consistent with the complexity of the task or the embedded content standards.)

Organization: Teachers must ask themselves, "Does this lesson have a presence of required elements, including the following: Subject(s), Grade Level(s), Goals, Objectives, Instructional Strategies, Procedures, and Assessment?" "Is there a logical relationship between the activities that will be implemented for this lesson and the objectives?"

Appropriateness: Teachers must ask themselves, "Does this lesson plan use appropriate tools, resources and information conflicts by validating information through research and comparison of data?"

> *Demonstrate knowledge of skills and strategies for collaborating effectively with colleagues to plan instruction.*

Some strategies for collaborating effectively on instruction include, but are not limited to, the following (excerpted from *www.wikihow.com/Collaborate–in–Lesson–Planning*):

- Choose a suitable time and place to meet, and choose the people you want to meet with. Stick to similar subject areas. A teacher of math and a teacher of drama may find it difficult to discuss common ground in lesson planning.

- Select a chairperson who will oversee collaboration. (This is only necessary if there will be a large number contributing. If there are fewer than five, no chairperson will be necessary.)

- Engage in a brainstorming session in which all ideas for classroom projects will be accepted. Write these down on a flipchart or whiteboard.

- Narrow down the ideas to decide on the top choices. Discuss how things could work or any problems that might be encountered with any of the ideas.

- Pull together the details of the project you've chosen, and write these down so that you can all have a copy of what has been agreed on. Either photocopy this or circulate it via e-mail.

- Consult administrators as to the feasibility of the project (consider things like cost and schedule space).

- Test out the project in classrooms. Perhaps each member of the staff could try out one of the ideas and then report back on the relative success at the end of the week.

- Reconvene and reflect on the process; discuss any problems you encountered or things that worked well. Refine your techniques and consider how to improve the techniques for next time.

- Implement the new teaching methods as permanent additions to your scheme of work or year plan.

Sample Questions for Competency 8

1. The most useful definition of *curriculum* is

   A. the academic offerings of the school.

   B. all the experiences in a child's life.

   C. the experiences, both planned and unplanned, that affect the education and growth of a child.

   D. all the educational experiences of a child, with the exception of extracurricula experiences.

2. Which of the following statements is NOT true of standards-based education and high-stakes tests based on those standards?

   A. A study of the Georgia assessment system found no evidence of teachers emphasizing whatever material they believed would raise test scores on the CRCT.

   B. Evidence suggests that elements of the curriculum not covered by these standards and tests are deemphasized.

   C. Teachers give priority to academic content covered by the tests.

   D. Evidence suggests that this approach encourages teachers to "teach to the test."

3.	A performance standard specifies which of the following:

   A.	The condition under which students demonstrate knowledge

   B.	The audience for which standards are created

   C.	What students should know and be able to do

   D.	The terminal expectation of student learning

4.	An Interdisciplinary Instructional Unit

   A.	is just a middle school thing.

   B.	allows two or more teachers to develop several lesson plans with a common theme and joint outcomes.

   C.	can be done only in a group or team approach.

   D.	are confusing for students to follow.

5.	In an era of standards-based instruction, teachers need to plan instruction

   A.	that begins with an interesting activity.

   B.	that is highly motivating for the entire class.

   C.	that is in the teacher's greatest content strength.

   D.	"backwards" from the standards.

Answers

1. **C**

2. **A**

3. **C**

4. **B**

5. **D**

Notes

1.	*www.georgiastandards.org/faqs.aspx*

2.	*www.edutopia.org/technology-integration-introduction*

3.	*http://712educators.about.com/cs/technology/a/integratetech.htm*

CHAPTER

Competency 9

Understand various instructional approaches
and principles of instruction and how to apply
this knowledge to provide students with effective
and appropriate learning experiences

Instructional Approaches and Principles of Instruction

The following instructional approaches will be discussed and defined to provide readers a key for the acquisition of knowledge:

Cooperative learning: An effective teaching strategy which involves forming small teams of students with varying levels of ability, and using an assortment of instructional activities. In this dynamic, students are not only responsible for learning the subject matter, but they are also responsible for their teammates' grasp of it. The team must work until all members understand the material and are able to complete the task. This method generates a feeling of achievement for everyone, since the students who are able to understand the material more quickly are given the added and more advanced task of helping their peers. (see *www.edtech.kennesaw.edu/intech/cooperativelearning.htm*).

Interdisciplinary instruction: As mentioned in the last chapter, interdisciplinary learning involves the simultaneous application of a theme, a problem, a principle, a process, an experience, or a value to more than one academic discipline. The organizational structure of interdisciplinary learning is built upon one theme (or unit). Upon this theme is constructed a framework of goals that specify what students will learn from the lessons that are a part of the unit. This method helps students appreciate the connections that exist among the disciplines. For examples of interdisciplinary instruction in action, see *www.thirteen.org/edonline/concept2class/interdisciplinary/index.html#sbs*.

Hands-on activities: Learning by doing. It enables students to become critical thinkers by being able to apply not only *what* they have learned but, more importantly, the *process of learning*, to various life situations.

Technology-based learning: Constitutes learning by electronic technology, including the Internet, intranets, satellite broadcasts, audio and video conferencing, bulletin boards, chat rooms, Webcasts, and CD-ROM. Technology-based learning also encompasses related terms, such as online learning and Web-based learning.

Guided discovery: A process that teachers use to introduce new materials, explore areas of the classroom, and prepare children for various aspects of the curriculum. Examples of times when a guided discovery lesson may be used include an introduction to using a thesaurus, the exploration of a book corner or computer center, or preparation for using choice time. This process gives children an opportunity to creatively and actively engage with the new tool or area, ask questions, and practice making appropriate choices with regard to the focus of the discovery.

Mastery learning: Mastery learning is a method of learning based on the theory that all children can learn efficiently when they are provided with appropriate learning conditions. In mastery learning, emphasis is removed from the lesson content, and directed instead toward the process through which the student masters it. This method is most easily applied to a traditional, content-focused curriculum in which the objectives are clearly defined, and organized in small, sequential units. Employed successfully, this method of learning will produce the same benefits of personal tutoring, and achieve throughout the whole class the independent working habits usually seen in only high-achieving students. In a mastery learning environment, the teacher employs a variety of group-based instructional activities, and provides precise feedback expediently in two ways: with the help of diagnostic and formative, criterion-referenced assessments; and by systematically correcting students' mistakes. (See *http://www.funderstanding.com/content/mastery-learning*).

The following direct instructional techniques promote student learning:

Lectures: Perhaps the most criticized of all teaching methods and also the most commonly used because planning time is limited and lectures are flexible and can be applied to any content. Lectures are also simple. The most critical fact about lecturing is that it puts students in a passive role.

Guided practice: This strategy is effective for teaching thinking skills as well as content. When teachers pose questions that will gradually lead students from easy or familiar examples to new understandings of the lesson, they are guiding practice. Teachers can also use guided practice to see that their students have grasped specific skills, concepts, and modeling that they may have presented to them. With guided practice, students are individually accountable for demonstrating what they understand.

Modeling: With this direct instructional technique, teachers model the desired behaviors or skill they want their students to master.

Following is the first of six skills required for meeting Competency 9.

Demonstrate knowledge of how to organize and implement instruction that promotes the ability of all students to achieve learning goals (e.g., using various grouping strategies; differentiating instruction; using multiple strategies for teaching the same content; using effective instructional resources and materials, including computers and other technological resources).

The differentiation of instruction allows educators to rethink traditional educational practices that were based on a time when students were more similar in background. Because of the vast diversity of students in our schools, educators today must embrace differentiated instruction for students and assume a confident attitude that they can effectively organize and manage this type of instruction. Differentiating instruction means creating several different avenues for students with varying aptitude, interests, or learning styles, to grasp, process, create, and express their ideas throughout the learning process. Students take ownership of their own education, and are given an opportunity to participate in peer teaching and cooperative learning. Differentiation can occur in the content, process, product, or environment in the classroom (see *http://members.shaw.ca/priscillatheroux/differentiating.html*).

Four ways to differentiate instruction, along with definitions, are as follows (excerpted from *www.members.shaw.ca/priscillatheroux/differentiating.html*):

1. *Differentiate the content or topic:* Content can be described as the knowledge, skills, and attitudes teachers want students to learn. Differentiating content requires that students are pretested so the teacher can identify the students who do not require direct instruction. Students demonstrating understanding of a concept can skip the instruction step and proceed to apply the concepts to the task of solving a problem. Another way to differentiate content is simply to permit the

apt students to accelerate their rate of progress. They can work ahead independently on some projects, as they cover the content faster than their peers.

2. *Differentiate the process or activity:* This means varying learning activities or strategies to provide appropriate methods for students to explore the concepts. It is important to give students alternative paths to manipulate the ideas embedded within the concept. For example, students may use graphic organizers, maps, diagrams, or charts to display their comprehension of concepts covered. Varying the complexity of the graphic organizer can facilitate differing levels of cognitive processing for students of differing ability.

3. *Differentiate the product:* This means varying the complexity of the product that students create to demonstrate mastery of the concepts. Students working below grade level may have reduced performance expectations, while students above grade level may be asked to produce work that requires more complex or more advanced thinking. There are many sources of alternative product ideas available to teachers. However, sometimes it is motivating for students to be offered a choice of product.

4. *Differentiate by manipulating the environment or accommodating individual learning styles:* Many classrooms offer limited opportunities to change the lighting or sound levels, to eliminate visual distracters, or to provide a more casual seating arrangement for students. Varying teaching strategies makes sure that students will occasionally learn in a manner compatible with their own learning preference but also expands their repertoire of alternative learning strategies in turn.

Very often, these learning strategies are used in conjunction with one another.

> *Evaluate the effectiveness of various methods for organizing and implementing a given lesson (e.g., strategies for introducing and closing a lesson, strategies for building on students' prior knowledge and experience).*

Strategies for opening a lesson include, but are not limited to, the following:

Opening Strategies (building on prior knowledge)

*   Identify the most important word from the previous lesson.

*   Give an example or illustration of yesterday's lesson.

    Contrast _____ with _____

    Describe _____

- Identify the relationship between a current event and the current week's topic.

- Apply a skill from the previous lesson to new information.

- Give students a multiple-choice item, then pair students and compare their answers.

- Assign a timed reading with written response (the reading selection should be related to the week's topics).

Exiting or Closing Strategies

- Have students write a report of what they learned (digest or log).

- Ask students to write questions about today's lesson; exchange questions.

- Implement exit tickets as a part of the school day. (Students answer the essential question of the day on a scrap of paper.)

> *Recognize the importance of continuously monitoring instructional effectiveness and responding flexibly to student understanding, engagement, and feedback (e.g., by changing the pace of a lesson, using a different instructional approach, taking advantage of an unanticipated learning opportunity).*

In order for students to self-assess their progress in class, teachers must provide relevant and steady feedback that provides guidance for students as they endeavor on their roads to learning. Teachers must always consider what methods are working while reinventing the methods that don't work and keeping the methods that do. Effective instruction includes the following principles taken from M. David Merrill (*edutechwiki.unique.ch/en/First_principles_of_instruction*):

The demonstration principle: Learning is promoted when learners observe a demonstration.

The application principle: Learning is promoted when learners apply the new knowledge.

The activation principle: Learning is promoted when learners activate prior knowledge or experience.

The integration principle: Learning is promoted when learners integrate their new knowledge into their everyday world.

The task-centered principle: Learning is promoted when learners engage in a task-centered instructional strategy.

Differentiated instructional strategies are needed to teach in today's classroom. In any given classroom, the diversity of the student population in a classroom will not permit traditional teaching practices. Diverse students bring many different experiences to today's classroom, giving great opportunities for unexpected or unanticipated learning opportunities. *Unanticipated learning* is defined as a spontaneous action or transaction, the intention of which is task accomplishment but which serendipitously increases particular knowledge, skill, or understanding. Unanticipated learning includes such things as learning from mistakes, learning by doing, learning through networking, and learning from a series of interpersonal experiments. With the vast diversity embodied inside of today's classroom, the experiences of students, as well as their natural inclination to learn, may take lessons to other levels. It is important that educators embrace these times as teachable moments, in order to enrich the whole class's learning experience.

> *Demonstrate knowledge of how to integrate computers and other technologies effectively into instruction.*

Technology is everywhere in our lives, and educators are obliged to keep up (see Becker, Mehlinger, and Sheingold & Hadley). Parents, teachers, administrators, and civil leaders have put as high priority the integration of technology in the classroom. However, the application of technology to classroom instruction has been overlooked (see Bryant and Cuban). To integrate technology into the classroom effectively, teachers must first be familiar with and able to use whatever technological advances their system or school provides.

Examples of strategies for integrating computers and other technologies into instruction are as follows (excerpted from *www.fno.org/oct04/integrating.html*):

- Use the Internet to view satellite photos of places described in novels and visit the chambers of commerce from those places to understand the social dynamics of the community and, therefore, the context of a novel.

- Use a spreadsheet to record times of travel between two cities, figuring in travel speeds, weather conditions, and distances, and represent the data in several graphical forms to gain an understanding of dependent and independent variables.

- Study sound wave patterns to examine harmonic patterns and learn about chord structure.

- Videotape students in hallways and use a spreadsheet to chart the length and number of interactions a student engages in, compared to his grade-point average.

- Use projectors for sharing a single computer connection with the entire class.

Technology helps students question, research, understand, analyze, evaluate, create, apply, and present, which are all aspects of the learning process. With every lesson, ask yourself, "How can technology help my students fulfill their objectives?"

Demonstrate knowledge of how to use effective instructional approaches (e.g., using graphic organizers, simulations, inquiry, role-playing, questioning) to promote the ability of students to acquire, analyze, and organize information, synthesize knowledge, and solve problems.

Teachers can help their students to classify ideas and communicate more effectively by using graphic organizers. Graphic organizers can be used in many ways, for example, structuring writing projects, helping in problem solving, aiding decision making, studying, planning research, and brainstorming. Visual thinking can be expressed in many ways. Graphic organizers are one way for visual thinkers to arrange their ideas. There are unlimited ways to express these visual ideas. Graphic organizers have many names like *visual maps*, *mind mapping*, and *visual organizers*. Although many students plan with paper and pencil, technology tools can be very helpful because they allow easy editing.

Graphic organizers can be used in all phases of learning, from brainstorming ideas to presenting findings. They can be used individually or in large groups. For example, some teachers like to create a class concept map as a large group to review at the end of a unit or develop a character map while reading a book aloud to the class. These tools are particularly useful in activities that require critical thinking skills.[1]

"A *simulation* is a form of experiential learning. Simulations are instructional scenarios in which the learner is placed in a "world" defined by the teacher and representing a reality within which students interact. The teacher controls the parameters of this world and uses it to achieve the desired instructional results. Simulations are similar to lab experiments in which the students themselves are the test subjects. Students experience the reality of the scenario and gather meaning from it. This strategy fits well with the principles of constructivism. Simulations promote the use of critical and evaluative thinking, as students are encouraged to contemplate the implications of a scenario. The situation feels real and thus leads to more engaging interaction by learners. Simulations can help students analyze and acquire knowledge. Through simulation, students get to delve into a view of the content that is abstract but will yield the same outcome that the teacher seeks, which is the acquisition of knowledge."[2]

> *Evaluate the appropriateness of various instructional approaches and learning resources (e.g., print resources, primary sources and artifacts, guest speakers, audiovisual materials, computer and other technological resources) for addressing instructional goals and responding to student learning needs.*

Many resources are needed to give students the best educational experiences. The use of print resources, artifacts, audiovisual materials, and other technological equipment only enhance the quality of education students receive in our schools. Different subjects have needs for different resources, in order to enrich the lesson. Every subject needs to address instructional goals, as well as respond to the learning needs of the students. A *learning goal* may be defined as a general statement of desired accomplishment. It does not specify exactly all of the components or steps or how each step will be achieved on the road to accomplishing the goal. By enriching the goals with the necessary resources, students have a better chance of retaining and acquiring knowledge. Good lessons are differentiated and involve more resources than paper and pencil.

Sample Questions for Competency 9

1. When students use computers in school, they receive all of the following advantages EXCEPT

    A.   enhanced social development.

    B.   immediate feedback.

    C.   increased motivation.

    D.   essential twenty-first century skills.

2. What type of learning provides students with opportunities to inquire into subjects so that they "discover" knowledge for themselves?

    A.   Mastery learning

    B.   Inquiry learning

    C.   Outcome-based learning

    D.   Contingency learning

3. Scaffolding is based on the works of

    A.   Vygotsky.

    B.   Glasser.

    C.   Greenberg.

    D.   Cantor.

4. Research on cooperative learning suggests that

    A.   it has a positive effect on the achievement of students of color.

    B.   students working together rarely develop positive attitudes about their classmates.

    C.   students are best served by participating in few roles and responsibilities.

    D.   this approach promotes racist attitudes.

5. Mr. Davis, a high school teacher, is chairperson of the curriculum development committee in math. His focus is on providing the facts, laws, and principles of math. He will most likely be advocating

    A.   a student-centered curriculum.

    B.   a college curriculum.

    C.   a subject-centered curriculum.

    D   an integrated curriculum.

Answers

1. **A**

2. **B**

3. **A**

4. **A**

5. **C**

Notes

1. *http://eduscapes.com/tap/topic73.htm*

2. *http:olc.spsd.sk.ca/DE/PD/instr/strats/simul/index.html*

CHAPTER

Competency 10

10

Understand how to promote positive, productive relationships among school, home, and community to support and enhance student learning and well-being

Promotion of Positive Relationships Among School, Home, and Community

Teachers are the force that will be able to do the following:

1. Promote positive relationships among school colleagues.

2. Promote a positive relationship between the school community and the parents/guardians in the homes of the students.

3. Promote a positive relationship between the school and the local community.

4. Promote positive relationships through sound ethical practice.

Their methods include demonstrating a knowledge of strategies for developing partnerships with parents/guardians to support student learning and academic achievement, including engaging families in a variety of school-based activities. Family involvement in a child's education is linked with success in school, according to a Harvard Family Research Project.

The school of today is very different from the school most of your parents attended and is probably different from the school you attended. Today's school children may come from single-parent families; many come from families made up of relatives, with no biological parent present. This is different from the father as the breadwinner and a stay-at-home mother to take care of child rearing. Many students come to school from the care of a guardian, not a parent. The students today may be sexually active at the middle school age and are emotionally drained by the pressure of peers and a society that dictates what is acceptable.

One cause of this phenomenon is the change in the structure of the American family. In 2000, only 6 percent of the total number of households had a father that worked and a mother who did not work outside the home (Kauchak & Eggen). Also in 2000, 70 percent of women with children were in the workforce. One out of four adults is a grandparent; 3.7 million children (5.1 percent of all children under 18) are living in a home maintained by grandparents (Morrison).

Students spend five times as much time in their neighborhoods and at home as they do in school, so this is where children learn about life, establish values, and develop attitudes. In 1966, the Coleman Report indicated that family background exerted a powerful influence on student learning (Coleman, et al.).

The federal No Child Left Behind Act (NCLB) has changed the way the State interacts with parents. Since the role of the parent is so crucial to success for the child, the State is mandated to involve the parents in their child's education. Before NCLB, the school district was responsible for the child's overall education. The Head Start Program for low-income children also requires parent involvement.

Four approaches have been identified for parent involvement during the last decade:

1. Parent Empowerment Approach: Moncrieff Cochran developed this approach, which focuses on strengthening the family by promoting the characteristics of a robust family.

2. Cultural Competence Approach: Luis Moll developed this approach, based on the premise that minority and low-socioeconomic status students benefit from family involvement.

3. Social Capital Approach: James Coleman developed this approach. Social capital in families is very important for children's intellectual development.

4. Functional Approach: Joyce Epstein based her approach on the six National PTA standards. (Morrison 192)

Responsibilities for the parent include the following:

- Have parents monitor student attendance.

- Have parents assist with homework.

- Create a homework website to inform parents of the schedule of homework.

- Monitor the amount of computer and TV time that is not related to school function.

- Volunteer to be a part of the child's educational process.

- Attend parent-teacher conferences on a regular basis.

- Read and respond to all reports that target the child's academic progress at school.

Responsibilities for the school include the following:

- Distribute accurate and timely information to parents about school functions and activities.

- Explain school-building and school-district rules and procedures for parents so they can explain them to their children.

- Provide access to textbooks for parents to help with homework.

- Create a master calendar for the parents that allows them to know in advance what is going on in the schools.

- Coordinate between all the schools in the district the schedule of outside events.

- Explain testing and assessment procedures and results to parents and community members.

- Provide parents information about the curriculum.

- Recognize the importance of communicating with families on a regular basis and analyzing strategies for initiating and maintaining effective communication with families.

Some of the ways to involve parents in the welfare of their child's education are to inform them of all aspects of the educational process:

- Family-centered programs focus on meeting the needs of students through the particular family arrangement the student is living in.

- Family-centered teaching focuses on helping both generations (students and parents) find success. This allows the teacher to address multiple issues that affect the family and the student, such as medical care, and allows the teacher to focus on cognitive and academic needs.

- Family-centered teaching can help individuals become better parents, help gain access to community resources, and assist in literacy for the entire family.

Schools cannot be effective without the involvement of parents. Research from the U.S. Department of Education indicates that students benefit from the communication between the home and the school.

The results of parental involvement include the following:

- Higher student achievement

- Higher grades and test scores

- Better class attendance; fewer absences

- More regular homework completion

- More positive attitudes toward school and schoolwork

- Lower incidence of alcohol and drug use, also lower incidence of teenage pregnancy

- Higher expectations for student success in school

The first of three skills required for mastering Competency 10 is as follows:

Identify effective strategies for addressing parents'/guardians' concerns in given situations, including conferences.

Effective schools involve parents and the rest of the community to help design school plans to better meet the learning and well-being needs of the students. In the United States, there are many different approaches to community schooling. The federal government does not have a national policy on education. The role of education has been left up to the states to decide on curriculum and all matters pertaining to education. Most schools have many opportunities for parents to be involved. One way is through the parent-teacher conference. This is a method of communicating with parents about their children's success or failure in school. The conference can encompass a number of topics from academics to behavior. It is also a time to assess the needs of the family for service from the school. The teacher can also schedule home visits. One growing area is the need to meet with and discuss the student's academic life with a language-minority parent or family. This may involve not only language difficulty but cultural and religious challenges as well.

One aspect of the NCLB Act is the *school choice* option when schools are not meeting standards. This allows families to choose the school the children will attend. There are both *public* and *private* schools in most communities, as well as the following types:

- *Pre-kindergarten* for most communities; characteristics are (1) shared cost, (2) enrollment by district, and (3) enrollment by application.

- *Kindergarten* in most communities: half-day and full-day.

- *Primary education* or *elementary school* in most communities:

    grades 1–6

    grades 1–3 (lower-elementary)

    grades 4–6 (upper-elementary)

    grades 1–8 (private school elementary)

- *Middle school education* is in most communities:

    grades 6–8 (standard model)

    grades 6–9 (with 6–7 as lower and 8–9 as upper)

- *High school education* is in most communities:

    grades 9–12

    grades 10–12

- *Alternative learning programs* are in most communities:

    Special needs students

    Students with problems (behavioral, legal, social)

    Special curriculum offerings (trade schools, vocational schools)

- There are urban, suburban, and rural schools:

    Urban schools: In cities, schools are rich in culture and diversity; students are local; possibly issues with poverty, older school buildings

    Suburban schools: Outside the cities, some diversity, less cultural heritage, more open space, poverty less of an issue, newer school buildings

    Rural schools: In the country, not near a city, students travel further to attend, very little diversity, very little cultural heritage, may have issues relating to poverty

Characteristics of a good community school are as follows:

- Parents play an active role in assisting their child's learning experience.

- Parents are encouraged to be actively involved in the education process.

- Parents are full partners in their child's education.

- Parents expect an emphasis on high standards and increased accountability.

- The community contributes to safe and secure school environment.

- All classrooms are staffed with qualified and competent, caring teachers.

> *Demonstrate knowledge of how to interact appropriately and effectively with all families.*

The teacher must understand diversity; issues include language, culture, gender, ability differences, and students with exceptionalities.

The teacher must also understand changes in the student population and student differences. Issues include homelessness, teenage pregnancy, obesity, homosexuality, bullying, and alcohol and drug use.

> *Demonstrate knowledge of resources in the community (e.g., cultural institutions, businesses, individuals, social service agencies) and strategies for using these resources to promote student development and learning.*

Community-based teaching allows the school and the teacher to refer parents and the student to social service agencies within the community. Many parents are unaware of these agencies and fail to take advantage of needed community services.

Schools can assist with parenting by offering parenting skills, family support, and encouragement. Many schools offer parenting classes in the evening.

Communicating with parents through a school-to-home and a home-to-school method will create a two-way channel that families can use. This creates a method for families to contact teachers and for teachers to contact families.

The school should coordinate the work and resources of the local community and make these available to members of the school family.

Teachers must recognize the different stakeholders in the community. These include local businesses (need an educated workforce), both state and national professional teacher organizations (maintain working conditions for teachers), community agencies (provide services), parents (legal responsibilities), and students (social development).

Sample Questions for Competency 10

1. How does involving parents contribute to a productive learning environment?

   A. Productive learning environments are disorderly and do not focus on learning.

   B. Research has shown that when parents are involved, there is a contribution to a safe, orderly learning environment.

   C. Productive learning environments are primarily a factor between the student and the teacher and do not include the parents.

   D. Productive learning environments are a function of classroom management only.

2. Which of the following would be an effective strategy for a teacher to communicate with parents?

   A. Parent-teacher conferences

   B. Open houses and reports sent home

   C. Report cards and progress reports

   D. All of the above

3. According to the NCLB Act of 2001, schools that perform poorly over a six-year period

   A. could receive funds for student tutoring.

   B. may have a name change.

   C. could be bypassed for any type of funding.

   D. none of the above

4. Thelma Farquar is a new and nervous kindergarten teacher preparing for her first set of parent conferences. Among the tasks she needs to attend to is

   A. set out comfortable chairs for parents across from her desk.

   B. put out fresh flowers and decorate the room.

   C. arrange side-by-side seating at a table.

   D. double-check her appointments.

5. A parent has left an angry message on a teacher's voice mail. The message relates to a concern about a student and is directed at the teacher. The teacher should

   A. call back immediately and confront the parent.

   B. cool off; plan what to discuss with the parent, then call back.

   C. question the student about what he said to the parent to cause the anger.

   D. ignore the whole thing.

Answers

1. **B**

2. **D**

3. **A**

4. **C**

5. **B**

Competency 11

Understand how to work effectively with colleagues; reflect productivity on one's own teaching practice; seek feedback from a variety of sources; and update and strengthen one's professional knowledge, skills, and effectiveness

Communication with Others in the Field of Education

The first of five skills needed to meet this competency is as follows:

Demonstrate knowledge of the roles and responsibilities of various members of the school community and methods for working effectively with others in the educational community to strengthen teaching knowledge, skills, and effectiveness.

The top of the educational hierarchy at the local level is the school committee or school board (also called a board of education). These individuals are usually elected from the community, and establish the policies by which a local educational system is run. They also have fiscal responsibility that involves managing the resources of the district so that they meet their responsibilities. They establish mission statements, goals, and objectives that are in accordance with community needs and desires, as well as state and local requirements. Of the most important roles this body has, its primary responsibility is the hiring and supervising of the district superintendent.

The district superintendent is the chief operating officer of the school district. It is his responsibility to oversee the day-to-day operations of the local schools. His or her job is to implement Board of Regents and school board policies and to be the primary advocate for the school district. The superintendent of schools recommends the hiring of all school personnel, oversees the creation of the yearly budget, supervises or oversees the supervision of all school personnel, and has primary responsibility for the success or failure of the school district.

GACE Tip

A school principal may have occasion to discipline faculty.

School principals are hired by the superintendent of schools to supervise and operate a school in the district. Their responsibility is to deal with all school management and supervisory functions and to be the lead in professional development of the school curriculum, practice, and strategies. School discipline is a significant role of the school principal. This discipline may involve faculty as well as students. The principal works under the direct supervision of the superintendent in all matters and, indirectly, under the school board.

Although Georgia is a "right to work" state, unions such as the AFT (American Federation of Teachers) and the NEA (National Education Association) are represented in the local districts. Although they don't have collective bargaining rights as they do in other states, they do provide significant professional development activities as do other professional organizations. Other organizations, such as the National Middle School Association (NMSA), ASCD (the Association of Supervision and Curriculum Development), and many others, are active agencies for teacher professional development and act as teacher activists and advocates for the profession.

Additional organizations, such as the PTA and PTO, act as parent advocates in the educational process. They allow parents access and a voice in their child's schools. They engage parents in the school-based decision process through school improvement teams and a wide variety of advisory councils. They are also agencies that promote and encourage parent-teacher cooperation.

> *Demonstrate knowledge of strategies for collaborating with specialists and others in the school community to enhance student learning.*

For beginning teachers, the strategy of assigning a mentor teacher is well ingrained in the educational system. These mentors are trained and selected to provide support to the beginning teacher in critical areas such as assessment, teaching strategies, and classroom management techniques. Their role is to develop the novice as a professional. Other members of our community of learners become important as a teacher grows into his career. Art, music, and exploratory-area teachers have much to teach in the way of holistic, integrated education. They are masters in the area of performance assessment and can bring both relevance and multiple intelligences to teaching skills.

Other educators, both peers and administrators, can provide direction as critical friends in our classrooms, offering nonjudgmental advice on their observation of our lessons, strategies, and practices. The sharing of promising practices is another way to grow the profession of education. Freely sharing what has worked well in the classroom and, conversely, warning of those techniques and practices that haven't worked well, are vitally important to building capacity in our schools.

Teachers need to remember that they are part of a team and that their success is part of the greater success that everyone hopes to achieve. Being open to and actively seeking growth opportunities are signs of a consummate professional.

> *Recognize effective strategies for using reflection and self-assessment to identify strengths, challenges, and potential problems for the purpose of improving teaching practice and achieving professional goals.*

The activity and practice of becoming a lifelong learner is of importance to continued growth as a professional educator. Teachers can and do become pedantic and boring when they stop growing. Teachers who have lost their passion become the primary reason so many of our students find little joy or motivation in their dreary classes. On the other hand, there are those who continue to grow and improve and who seek formal and informal educational pathways to keep their passion alive. They believe that learning never ends. They constantly reflect on their teaching and improve it so that it is never the same, always growing. These teachers grow our success rate. They engage and excite students. They encourage and collaborate with their peers.

Successful teachers are self-reflectors and self-assessors. They not only evaluate the success of their strategies, they evaluate their personal skills and growth. These teachers look for role models to emulate. They measure their successes on a yearly basis by their students' successes. These teachers encourage and listen to feedback from both students and peers as an important element in their own growth. They also engage in formal education periodically to see how they measure up to others' expectations.

> *Demonstrating knowledge of how to use a variety of professional development opportunities and resources to enhance professional knowledge, skills, and expertise.*

Physicians and attorneys refer to their work as "a practice" because with each patient and each case they are improving their ability to work within their disciplines. Teaching isn't referenced that way, but it remains true that for each student and each class taught, teachers refine their skills. Professional development further refines these skills. We may examine professional development in three venues: (1) continued learning, (2) mentoring, and (3) research. Together they represent a teacher's activities that are directed toward being a part of and a contributor to the discipline of education.

1. As learners, teachers pursue their professional growth through formal coursework. Today, retaining teacher certification requires continued education through the additional coursework of a college or university or the accumulation of CEUs (continuing education units) or PDUs (professional development units). As this latter path is far less expensive than college tuition, it is often preferred by junior teachers. Many teachers today retain certification through the CEU/PDU route; however, many decide to complete recertification requirements by earning advanced degrees. An advantage to traveling the advanced-degree route is that salary increases are often tied to the degrees.

GACE Tip

Salary increases are often tied to degrees earned.

Some professional development opportunities do not involve coursework, nor are they tied to recertification requirements or degree programs. School districts often provide in-service programs and workshops for teachers at their schools. These in-service programs are often tied to district or school goals. Their intent is not to increase a teacher's subject-area knowledge as much as it is to keep the teachers learning; along with learning is the awareness of what it is like to learn. That awareness, as well as the vibrancy of learning something new, is what districts hope that teachers will bring back to their classrooms. Even more productive for district in-service is a coordinated districtwide focus for the implementation of a coordinated effort to meet the needs of all students.

2. Mentoring of other teachers is part of the professional growth process. This special one-on-one educational experience is not the same as regular teaching. To be successful at this, the mentor must possess, among other things, patience, experience, and knowledge of teaching that goes deeper than the mere mechanics of instruction. Mentoring provides an individual with an opportunity to find her own style with the benefits of another's insight.

3. The final insight into the realm of professional development is in the area of research. Increasingly, we have come to view the classroom as valuable research territory for educational improvement. The close collaboration

of colleges of education with local schools, either as PDSs (professional development schools) or through partnerships like Holmes/Unite, have generated a "teacher-as-researcher" model. As an active partner in research efforts, the teacher raises his or her own level of professionalism by contributing to the accumulated body of educational knowledge. This creates new insights for teachers about teaching and learning. It also engages them in other professional activities in a supported atmosphere. Activities such as grant writing and giving presentations, which earlier might have been frightening and far too time consuming, become engaging activities.

This form of professional development may not be for everyone; however, a teacher-as-researcher collaboration offers professional development that is significantly different from coursework and mentoring in that it specifically focuses on bringing new knowledge to the field of education. It also provides avenues for the dissemination of this knowledge as presenter, author, or conference speaker. All are highly motivating and rewarding avenues for the experienced professional to travel in the pursuit of improving professional knowledge, skills, and expertise.

> *Demonstrate knowledge of formal and informal teacher observations and assessments and recognize ways to use feedback to strengthen one's own teaching skills and solve problems.*

"Everyone's a critic"—or so it appears to the classroom teacher. All those negative articles in the newspapers, the complaints of students, parents who are critical of everything, grumpy administrators, and even a spouse, all have something to say about a teacher's performance. Let's look at this assessment. Formal teacher assessments are done by a supervisor on a yearly basis. There are the critical comments of mentors, or "critical friends." Then there are the spurious comments made in anger, from frustration or jealousy by peers, parents, or even students. In every critical comment there is a kernel of truth. Observation by supervisors, and the comments of mentors and of critical friends are probably closest to objective reality and need careful reflection, along with an answer to the question, "What do I do next time to make it better?" It is necessary to be as dispassionate and objective about these criticisms as possible. Do not take them as personal attacks. They are, in fact, an opportunity for professional growth. Teachers can't improve if they don't know what needs improving. Once they are aware of needs or issues, specific advice from department heads, administrators, professional journals, or peers can be solicited to resolve the problem.

The less professional critics, such as parents, students, and others, should not be totally disregarded, however. Neither should teachers become impatient with or angry over them. It is best to thank people for their thoughts and indicate that you will take them into consideration. This approach calms the discussion and allows you to reflect at a later time—perhaps with colleagues—about how a lesson or situation could have been approached for a more successful outcome.

Professional development in all of its aspects and in every stage of a teacher's career contributes to healthy growth and professional strength.

Sample Questions for Competency 11

1. The superintendent of schools is responsible for

    A. signing the teachers' paychecks.

    B. making policies for the school district.

    C. the day-to-day operation of the schools in the district.

    D. supervising teachers.

2. The Parent Teacher Organization in any school is responsible for

    A. the quality of the food in the cafeteria.

    B. the access to and voice of parents in the school.

    C. raising money for playground equipment through bake sales and raffles.

    D. supervising the principal.

3. A social studies teacher in grade 7 is collaborating with the family and consumer science teacher to offer a unit on "Foods of the Middle Ages." This holistic approach to teaching can be considered a form of

    A. lunacy.

    B. professional development.

    C. laziness.

    D. experimental behavior.

4. The best way to address critical comments from a parent is to

A. ignore it.

B. argue the pedagogic truth to your methods, using as many statistics as possible.

C. call for an administrator to intervene before it becomes heated.

D. thank the parents for their thoughts and let them know you will take them into consideration.

5. The best form of professional development for a novice teacher is

A. learning through formal and informal means, mentoring, and action research.

B. formal coursework only.

C. CEUs or PDUs—only because of the cost involved.

D. mentors only because of the time involved.

Answers

1. **C**

2. **B**

3. **B**

4. **D**

5. **A**

Competency 12

12

Understand the rights and responsibilities of students, parents/guardians, teachers, and other school personnel in various educational contexts and the legal and ethical guidelines for educators in Georgia

Rights, Responsibilities, and Ethical Guidelines for Educators in Georgia

The first of seven skills needed to meet this competency is as follows:

Demonstrate knowledge of student rights and responsibilities in various contexts (due process, confidentiality, discipline, privacy, free speech, discrimination, harassment, compliance with school policy).

Tinker v. Des Moines Independent Community School District, 393 U.S. 503 (1969), brought the modern era of rights and responsibilities into focus. The resolution of this case was that a student did not shed his or her civil rights at the schoolhouse door. These rights may be infringed upon by school officials only when the expression of their rights would interfere with the operation of the school and the rights of other students to learn.

A later case, *Bethel School District v. Fraser,* 478 U.S. 675 (1986), modified the stark aspect of *Tinker* by ruling that a student's freedoms must meet the boundaries of socially appropriate behavior. The school then is recognized as having a basic educational mission and must be responsive to community values. Student behavior must fall within those two guidelines. Students must not interfere with the educational mission of the school or violate the community's values. In return, students are granted all of their civil rights, and the school's officials are bound to protect those rights.

Having noted all this, school officials are still given wide latitude in ensuring that the educational mission is not compromised. Locker and bag searches for the health and safety of all students are an accepted part of public school life.

Federal laws have further affected this area, with issues such as FERPA (Family Educational Rights and Privacy Act), making confidentiality a concern for teachers and school officials. Under these regulations a student's records are open only to those who have a need to know. Bullying can now be viewed as a form of discrimination, as can sexual harassment, both issues now of civil rights. In all cases involving students, clear and appropriate guidelines must be established and followed to avoid issues of due process. Due process is available to every student under the equal protection clause of the Fifth and Fourteenth Amendments of the U.S. Constitution.

> *Demonstrate knowledge of teacher rights and responsibilities in various contexts (e.g., in relation to students with exceptionalities, suspected abuse, safety issues, due process).*

Teachers have rights as citizens under the Constitution, just as students do; however, their professional practice is affected by their responsibilities as well as their rights. Teachers sit *in loco parentis* (in the place of a parent) in regard to their students. How far teachers may go in carrying out this parental function is an area of continuing controversy. Teachers in this role are responsible for discipline, supervision, guidance, and education of their charges in a reasonable and appropriate manner.

Teachers' rights include the following:

1. Nondiscrimination in pay, hiring, dismissal, promotion, and demotion (based on race, sex, creed, age, or sexual orientation)

2. Tenure, which is the right to permanent employment after serving a probationary period of from three to five years of successful teaching

3. Academic freedom, which is the right to teach subjects in the way the teacher wants and express views on these subjects within the bounds of community acceptability—that is, not disruptive to, or detrimental to, the educational process

Teachers' responsibilities include the following:

1. Uphold a duty and standard of care that includes providing a safe environment, providing proper instruction, and supervising students.

2. Always act in such a manner that the teacher can pass the "reasonable and prudent person" test.

3. Report suspected child abuse through the proper channels.

4. Avoid sexual harassment in word or deed.

5. Practice ethical behavior, as expressed by the district in school policy or that of professional organizations such as the NEA.

6. Observe all appropriate copyright laws.

Demonstrate knowledge of the rights and responsibilities of parents/guardians (e.g., in relation to student records, student attendance).

In an age when we expect greater parent participation in our schools and despair at the poor involvement of many parents in their child's education, parents' rights and responsibilities are poorly understood. The rights and responsibilities of parents/guardians include the following:

1. Parents have the right to be informed of their child's school progress and behavior.

2. Parents have the right to require informed consent before their child engages in school activities. This includes parental consent to field trips, disciplinary procedures, and certain curricula matters (sex education).

3. Parents must give consent for evaluation of a child for special education.

4. Parents have the right to examine all relevant documents pertaining to their child (evaluation, identification, or placement).

5. Parents have the right to present complaints concerning evaluation, placement, and identification of their child.

6. Parents may participate in the development of their child's IEP and must be informed in writing of any proposed change to placement, identification, or evaluation. Meetings to develop IEPs are to be set at a convenient time and place for the parents.

Parent/guardian responsibilities include the health, welfare, and education of their children. The most contentious element of this is often the parents' responsibility to ensure that their child is in school every day that the school is in session. (Compulsory attendance laws are in all states.) Parents may have their children attend private school, and a growing number of parents are home schooling their children. In all cases, an acceptable program of studies must be in place for this to occur.

> *Demonstrate knowledge of responsibilities and legal requirements associated with initiating, developing, and implementing Individualized Education Programs (IEPs).*

In 1975 the Education of All Handicapped Children Act (PL 94-142) was passed, providing for the education of all children in the least restrictive environment. In 1990 it was renamed as the Individuals with Disabilities Education Act (PL101–476). IDEA defines students with special needs as those with mental retardation, hearing impairments, speech or language impairments, serious emotional disturbance, orthopedic impairments, autism, traumatic brain injury, other health impairments, or specific learning disabilities. Up to 15 percent of our nation's students fall into these categories. Their concerns are addressed in each school system through a legal and binding contract with the school system called an IEP (Individualized Education Program).

IDEA has basic principles that address how educational services will be provided to these students and how these students are identified:

1. IDEA requires that an appropriate education be available to all students.

2. IDEA requires that a fair and creditable evaluation be used to determine if a student qualifies for services. It must be culturally and linguistically free of discrimination.

3. Various methods of evaluation must be used to determine whether a child qualifies for services. This requires the use of a Multi-disciplinary Team (MDT) to do the evaluation (psychologist, social worker, and so on).

4. An appropriate educational approach must be designed for the IEP. It must adequately address the student's needs in terms of maturity level, handicapping condition, age, past achievements, and parental expectations.

5. Education must be offered in the least restrictive environment for the nature of the students' handicap, as well as academic, social, and physical needs.

6. IDEA provides for procedural due process to resolve differences between the school system and the parents.

Students are referred to this process by a parent, teacher, school official, or a doctor or other professional. Referral is followed by a school-developed process of assessing student eligibility and educational needs involving the MDT. Parents and students (when appropriate) collaborate with school personnel to develop the IEP and determine the least restrictive environment within which this plan will be accomplished. This process now addresses students between the ages of three and twenty-one. As mentioned earlier, the elements of the IEP are a binding contract, by which teachers must abide.

> *Demonstrate knowledge of policies and procedures described in the Georgia Professional Standards Commission Code of Ethics for Educators.*

The Georgia code of ethics for educators contains ten standards. Under these standards, an individual who is in violation may have his or her certificate revoked, denied, or suspended. PSC may also issue a reprimand or warning, or may monitor an educator's conduct and performance. The following are grounds for disciplinary action: unethical conduct, as outlined in the Code of Ethics, disciplinary action in another state, an order from a court or other state agency, default on student loans, and any other good and sufficient cause, as judged by the PSC.

The standards in the Code of Ethics are as follows:

1. **Criminal acts.** Unethical conduct includes the commission or conviction of a felony or any crime involving moral turpitude.

2. **Abuse of students.** Unethical conduct includes any act of child abuse (physical or verbal); cruelty to children or any act of endangerment; any unlawful sexual acts; harassing behavior; having a written, verbal, or physical relationship with a student; the provision of or allowing the consumption of alcohol or drugs by a student.

3. **Alcohol or drugs.** Unethical behavior includes being on school premises or at a school-sponsored event while under the influence of, consuming, or being in possession of alcohol or illegal or unauthorized drugs.

4. **Misrepresentation or falsification.** Unethical conduct includes falsifying, or in other ways misrepresenting professional qualifications, criminal backgrounds, or employment history.

5. **Public funds and property.** Unethical conduct includes misusing public or school funds, failing to account for funds, fraud, commingling public and personal funds, using school property without approval.

6. **Improper remunerative conduct.** Unethical conduct includes soliciting funds or services that financially benefit an educator without prior approval, accepting gifts from vendors, accepting funds for tutoring or coaching, and promoting athletic camps to students for money unless under prior approval.

7. **Confidential information.** Unethical conduct includes the sharing of confidential information of a student's academic or disciplinary records, personal confidences, health and medical information, family status or income, and assessment testing results unless disclosure is required or permitted by law. This includes the sharing of standardized testing questions.

8. **Abandonment of contract.** Unethical conduct includes refusing to perform services required by a contract or abandoning the contract prior to release by the employer.

9. **Failure to make a required report.** Unethical conduct includes failure to report all information on documents required by the PSC, failure to report violations to the code of ethics, and failure to report child abuse.

10. **Professional conduct.** Unethical conduct is any conduct that impairs the certificate holder's ability to function professionally in his or her employment position or a pattern of behavior or conduct that is detrimental to the health, welfare, discipline, or morals of students.

> *Demonstrate familiarity with legal and ethical requirements regarding the use of educational resources and technologies (e.g., copyright laws, software piracy, acceptable use policies).*

With modern technology, teachers have access to many resources that are available to supplement their teaching. These resources include written works, graphics and photos, music, sculpture, movies and audiovisual works, drama, and sound recordings, — all available at the touch of a button. The use of this material is often governed by the Copyright Laws of 1978 and its subsequent amendments. These requirements include the following:

1. Teachers may make single copies of materials for their own use, as in research.

2. They may make multiple copies for their class or course, as long as the copyright appears on the copies.

3. Photocopies are not permitted where the material will replace a book used in the course or a consumable product such as a workbook.

4. Copies of software are governed by the licensing agreement under which it was purchased.

5. Advance permission must be received to copy a TV broadcast.

6. The basic issue is what constitutes "fair use." Materials may be used with some limits as long as they do not harm the market.

7. The amount of the resource used is an issue in fair use. Generally, no more than 10 percent of a work may be used without permission from the copyright holder.

> *Demonstrate familiarity with the roles and responsibilities of different components of the public education system in Georgia (e.g., boards of education, Georgia Professional Standards Commission).*

As in most states, elected officials direct the public school system of Georgia. At the local level, boards of education are elected by the citizens of each district. A key role of this board is to hire and supervise the superintendent of schools. In addition, the board sets policy and approves the curriculum and budget based on the superintendent's recommendation. The superintendent of schools oversees the day-to-day operation of the schools in the district and is responsible to the board of education for the success of those schools in educating the children of the community.

Note that the *board of education* is elected, and the *superintendent of schools* is hired. The state superintendent of schools is an elected official who convenes the appointed State Board of Education. This board sets state policy regarding education and submits it through the state superintendent to the legislature for action. The state superintendent acts as the chief educational advisor to the governor and the state legislature. The State Board of Education also acts as the board of appeals for actions taken at the local school-board level.

The PSC (Professional Standards Commission) is a separate state agency that sets standards, provides for teacher licensure (certification regulations), and is the state accrediting agency for schools and colleges of education.

Sample Questions for Competency 12

1. You have heard a young teenage boy in your homeroom talking about suicide with other students. What do you do?

   A. Talk to the boy, and let him know you will be speaking to his parents about this incident.

B.   Report this immediately to the school psychologist.

C.   Report this immediately to your principal or assistant principal. Make your own report to authorities if required by school or district policy. Do nothing else.

D.   Ignore the incident. Teenage boys are always looking for attention.

2.   The No Child Left Behind Act requires all teachers to be

A.   highly qualified.

B.   highly professional.

C.   highly intelligent.

D.   highly educated.

3.   You are a guest at a dinner party, and one of the other guests asks your opinion of the academic performance of their neighbor's son, who is in your class. You should

A.   explain what a good student the boy is and how he could get into a good college with a bit more effort.

B.   politely explain that you do not discuss your students except with their parents and the student himself.

C.   leave the party immediately.

D.   tell an amusing anecdote concerning the boy in class.

4.   A member of the board of education stops you on the street, and during the conversation she complains about another teacher in your school. You should

A.   call the teacher immediately and warn him that the board of education is out to get him.

B.   inform your principal.

C.   stop the board member and politely suggest that this is not the appropriate place for this discussion; rather, it should be taken up with the board and the superintendent of schools.

D.   keep the conversation to yourself.

5.   You have a workbook that students use in your classroom. Rather than order more copies and have less money in your budget for other things you wish to order, you

A.   make 40 copies for your class on the teacher's copy machine and use the copies instead.

    B.   tell your students not to write in the workbooks but to use a notebook for the answers.

    C.   drop the workbook from your teaching strategy and use another technique or resource.

    D.   make copies of the pages you use each day; at the end of the year, the students, in effect, have a complete workbook.

Answers

1. **C**

2. **A**

3. **B**

4. **C**

5. **C**

References

Anastasi, A. (1976). *Psychological Testing* (4th ed.). New York: McMillan.

Arends, R. I., & Winitzky, N. E. (2001). Instructor's Manual and Test Bank to accompany *Learning to Teach*. New York: McGraw-Hill Higher Education.

Arends, R. I., Winitzky, N. E., & Tannenbaum, M. D. (2001). Instructor's Manual and Test Bank to accompany *Exploring Teaching*. New York: McGraw-Hill Higher Education.

Becker, H. J. (2001). *How Are Teachers Using Computers in Instruction?* (Available at *www.crito.uci.edu*)

Bloom, B. S. (Ed.) (1956). *Taxonomy of Educational Objectives: The Classification of Educational Goals.* Handbook I: Cognitive Domain. Committee of College and University Examiners. New York: David McKay.

Bond, L. (1996). *Norm and Criterion Reference Materials,* p. 1. ERIC Clearinghouse on Assessment and Evaluation. (Available at *http://ericae.net/pare/getvn.asp?v=5&n=2*)

Brookhart, S. M. (2008). *How to Give Effective Feedback to Your Students.* Alexandria, VA: Association for Supervision and Curriculum Development.

Bryant, A. L. (2001). "Investment in Education and Technology: The Key to Preparing for the Digital Age." In *Techno: Quarterly for Education and Technology.* Winter. (Retrieved Nov. 19, 2008)

Burke, K. (2008). *What To Do With the Kid Who . . . Developing Cooperation, Self-Discipline, and Responsibility in the Classroom* (3rd ed.). Thousand Oaks, CA: Corwin Press.

Chapman, C., & Gregory, G. (2002). *Differentiated Instructional Strategies: One Size Doesn't Fit All.* Thousand Oaks, CA: Corwin Press.

Coleman, J., Campbell, E., Hobson, D., McPortland, J., Mood, A., Weinfield, F., & York, R. (1966). *Equality of Educational Opportunity.* Washington, DC: U.S. Department of Health, Education, and Welfare.

Cuban, L. (2001). *Oversold and Underused: Computers in the Classroom.* Cambridge, MA: Harvard University Press.

Davis, B. G. (1993). *Diversity and Complexity in the Classroom: Considerations of Race, Ethnicity, and Gender.* (Retrieved from *http://teaching.berkeley.edu/bgd/diversity.html*)

Ducharme, M. K., & McCartney, C. E. Instructor's Resource Manual with Test Bank to accompany *Foundations of Education: The Challenge of Professional Practice.* Needham Heights, MA: Allyn & Bacon.

Eccles, J. S. *The Development of Children Ages 6 to 1.* (Retrieved from *www.futureofchildren. org/information2827/information_show.htm?doc_id=71894*)

Erikson, E. H. (1968). *Identity: Youth and Crisis.* New York: W. W. Norton.

Gardener, H. (1989). *To Open Minds: Chinese Clues to the Dilemma of Contemporary Education.* New York: Basic Books.

Georgia Assessments for Certification of Educators (2008). Amherst, MA: Pearson Education Inc. (Available at *www.gace.nesinc.com/*)

Eysenck, M. W. *Adolescence, Adulthood and Old Age.* (Retrieved from *www.psypress.com/ pip/resources/chapters/PIP_adolescence.pdf*)

Jacobsen, D., Eggen P., and Kauchak, D. (2006). *Methods for Teaching: Promoting Student Learning in K-12 Classrooms.* Upper Saddle River, NJ: Pearson, Merrill Prentice Hall.

Johns, B. H. (2005). *Getting Behavioral Interventions Right: Proper Uses to Avoid Common Abuses.* Horsham, PA: LRP Publication.

Kauchak, D., and Eggen, P. (2008). *Introduction to Teaching: Becoming a Professional* (3rd ed.). Upper Saddle River, NJ: Pearson, Merrill Prentice Hall.

Marzano, R. J. (2003). *What Works in Schools: Translating Research Into Action.* Alexandria, VA: Association for Supervision and Curriculum Development.

Marzano, R. J. Pickering, D., & Pollock, J. (2001). *Classroom Instruction that Works: Research-Based Strategies for Increasing Student Achievement.* Association for Supervision and Curriculum Development.

Mehlinger, H. D. (1996). "School Reform in the Information Age." *Phi Delta Kappan,* 400–407.

Morrison, G. (2008). *Teaching in America* (5th ed.). Upper Saddle River, NJ: Pearson.

No Child Left Behind Act of 2001 (NCLB), Pub. L. 107-110 (8 January 2002). Washington, DC: U.S. Government Printing Office.

Nuttall, P. (1991). *Middle Childhood Development.* Family Day Care Facts Series. (Retrieved from *www.nncc.org/Child.Dev/mid.dev.html#anchor235923*)

Rhode, G., Jenson, W. R., & Reavis, H. K. (1993). *The Tough Kid Book: Practical Classroom Management Strategies.* Longmont, CO: Sopris West.

Sheingold, K., & Hadley, M. (1990). *Accomplished Teachers: Integrating Computers into Classroom Practices.* New York: Bank Street College of Education, Center for Technology in Education.

Shorall, C. P. (2004). *Pass the Praxis: The Principles of Learning and Teaching.* Upper Saddle River, NJ: Pearson Education, Inc.

Starr, L. (2005). "Understanding Kids Who Are Different: Activities for Teaching About Disabilities." *Education World*. (Retrieved from *www.educationworld.com/a_lesson/lesson115.shtml*)

State of Georgia Professional Services Commission, *GACE Exam Practice Tests* (Available at *www.gaceexampracticetests.com/*)

Thompson, M. (2000). "Scarcity of good paying jobs drives many to head north." *San Jose Mercury News*. Sept. 10.

Trumbull, E., & Pacheco M. (2005). "Leading with Diversity." The Education Alliance at Brown University. (Retrieved from *www.alliance.brown.edu/pubs/leading_diversity/lwd_introduction.pdf*)

U.S. Department of Commerce Economics and Statistics Administration. U.S. Census Bureau ACS-04 *American Community Survey Reports,* issued February 2000. (Retrieved from *www.census.gov/prod/2007pubs/acs-04.pdf*)

Wynne, S. A. (2007). *Professional Pedagogy* 171, 172. XAMonline, Inc., Melrose, MA.

Zirkel, P. A. (2001). *A Digest of Supreme Court Decisions Affecting Education*. Bloomington, IN: Phi Delta Kappa Educational Foundation.

Practice Test 1

GACE Professional Pedagogy
(Code 171)

ANSWER SHEET FOR PRACTICE TEST 1 (CODE 171)

1. Ⓐ Ⓑ Ⓒ Ⓓ

2. Ⓐ Ⓑ Ⓒ Ⓓ

3. Ⓐ Ⓑ Ⓒ Ⓓ

4. Ⓐ Ⓑ Ⓒ Ⓓ

5. Ⓐ Ⓑ Ⓒ Ⓓ

6. Ⓐ Ⓑ Ⓒ Ⓓ

7. Ⓐ Ⓑ Ⓒ Ⓓ

8. Ⓐ Ⓑ Ⓒ Ⓓ

9. Ⓐ Ⓑ Ⓒ Ⓓ

10. Ⓐ Ⓑ Ⓒ Ⓓ

11. Ⓐ Ⓑ Ⓒ Ⓓ

12. Ⓐ Ⓑ Ⓒ Ⓓ

13. Ⓐ Ⓑ Ⓒ Ⓓ

14. Ⓐ Ⓑ Ⓒ Ⓓ

15. Ⓐ Ⓑ Ⓒ Ⓓ

16. Ⓐ Ⓑ Ⓒ Ⓓ

17. Ⓐ Ⓑ Ⓒ Ⓓ

18. Ⓐ Ⓑ Ⓒ Ⓓ

19. Ⓐ Ⓑ Ⓒ Ⓓ

20. Ⓐ Ⓑ Ⓒ Ⓓ

21. Ⓐ Ⓑ Ⓒ Ⓓ

22. Ⓐ Ⓑ Ⓒ Ⓓ

23. Ⓐ Ⓑ Ⓒ Ⓓ

24. Ⓐ Ⓑ Ⓒ Ⓓ

25. Ⓐ Ⓑ Ⓒ Ⓓ

26. Ⓐ Ⓑ Ⓒ Ⓓ

27. Ⓐ Ⓑ Ⓒ Ⓓ

28. Ⓐ Ⓑ Ⓒ Ⓓ

29. Ⓐ Ⓑ Ⓒ Ⓓ

30. Ⓐ Ⓑ Ⓒ Ⓓ

31. Ⓐ Ⓑ Ⓒ Ⓓ

32. Ⓐ Ⓑ Ⓒ Ⓓ

33. Ⓐ Ⓑ Ⓒ Ⓓ

34. Ⓐ Ⓑ Ⓒ Ⓓ

35. Ⓐ Ⓑ Ⓒ Ⓓ

36. Ⓐ Ⓑ Ⓒ Ⓓ

37. Ⓐ Ⓑ Ⓒ Ⓓ

38. Ⓐ Ⓑ Ⓒ Ⓓ

39. Ⓐ Ⓑ Ⓒ Ⓓ

40. Ⓐ Ⓑ Ⓒ Ⓓ

41. Ⓐ Ⓑ Ⓒ Ⓓ

42. Ⓐ Ⓑ Ⓒ Ⓓ

43. Ⓐ Ⓑ Ⓒ Ⓓ

44. Ⓐ Ⓑ Ⓒ Ⓓ

45. Ⓐ Ⓑ Ⓒ Ⓓ

46. Ⓐ Ⓑ Ⓒ Ⓓ

47. Ⓐ Ⓑ Ⓒ Ⓓ

48. Ⓐ Ⓑ Ⓒ Ⓓ

49. Ⓐ Ⓑ Ⓒ Ⓓ

50. Ⓐ Ⓑ Ⓒ Ⓓ

51. Ⓐ Ⓑ Ⓒ Ⓓ

52. Ⓐ Ⓑ Ⓒ Ⓓ

53. Ⓐ Ⓑ Ⓒ Ⓓ

54. Ⓐ Ⓑ Ⓒ Ⓓ

55. Ⓐ Ⓑ Ⓒ Ⓓ

56. Ⓐ Ⓑ Ⓒ Ⓓ

57. Ⓐ Ⓑ Ⓒ Ⓓ

58. Ⓐ Ⓑ Ⓒ Ⓓ

59. Ⓐ Ⓑ Ⓒ Ⓓ

60. Ⓐ Ⓑ Ⓒ Ⓓ

Practice Test 1 (Code 171)

Directions: Read each question carefully, and circle the best response. Then, use the answer sheet and darken the circle that corresponds to the correct answer. Be cautious that the question number and the circle you are darkening are the same number.

1. A new teacher has been assigned to a school whose students come from a wide range of economic circumstances. Students from some neighborhoods typically have access to few cultural or educational resources, while students from other neighborhoods have access to an abundance of such resources. The teacher should be aware that students from these different circumstances are likely to differ from one another most in their

   A. preferred approaches to learning.

   B. background knowledge and experience.

   C. general aptitude for learning.

   D. level of motivation and task commitment.

2. Which of the following is the most important first step for a teacher to take in promoting students' ability to learn a skill through observation?

   A. Identify for students the most challenging aspects of the demonstrated skill.

   B. Describe verbally for students the sequence of steps that will occur in the demonstrated skill.

   C. Ensure that the students' attention is focused on the critical features of the demonstrated skill.

   D. Provide students with examples of real-world applications of the demonstrated skill.

3. A new teacher has been assigned to a class with a large number of English Language Learners. In working with students with linguistically diverse backgrounds, the teacher can best promote learning for all students in the class by

   A. having students with similar levels of English proficiency work together in small group activities.

   B. using questioning techniques that allow students to respond with brief correct or incorrect answers.

   C. adopting a consistent format for introducing important lesson concepts to students.

   D. providing students with frequent opportunities to talk, write, and read about instructional content.

4. Which of the following factors should be a teacher's primary consideration when planning the physical arrangement of the classroom?

   A. The range and distribution of student achievement levels

   B. The nature of the content and skills to be taught

   C. The types of learning activities the teacher plans to use

   D. The level of social interaction the teacher wishes to promote

5. Which of the following strategies is likely to be most effective for promoting positive interdependence among students in a small group activity?

   A. Requiring group members to share materials to complete the task

   B. Having group members evaluate one another's participation and contributions

   C. Specifying that group members will turn in a single product

   D. Creating complex tasks that require group members to rely on one another for information

6. A history teacher often presents content to students in narrative form, featuring vivid descriptions of inspiring historical figures struggling to accomplish great feats or right social wrongs. Which of the following best describes the outcome of this strategy?

    A.   Students are able to make their own connections across disciplines, deepening their understanding of broad concepts.

    B.   Students are led to use their own imaginations, fostering their ability to use creative thinking skills.

    C.   Content becomes more interesting and accessible to students, increasing their engagement with the subject matter.

    D.   Content becomes more relevant to students' own lives, increasing their ability to recall factual information.

7. You are going to use cooperative learning for the first time with your class. In creating the groups, you decide

    A.   to allow students to select their own groups.

    B.   to put all the behavior problems in one group so you can keep an eye on them.

    C.   to create groups balanced by ability and learning style.

    D.   to have students draw group numbers from a hat.

8. A team of teachers wants to use an interdisciplinary approach to instruction for an upcoming unit. What is the most important first step in planning this type of instructional unit?

    A.   Develop global questions to define the scope of the unit.

    B.   Identify activities to support students' understanding of unit content.

    C.   Create rubrics for evaluating student progress.

    D.   Define a single set of unit objectives that can be applied across the unit.

9. Because of their excitement about an upcoming holiday, the fourth-grade students in Mrs. Rahimi's class are having trouble focusing on the writing activity. In this situation Mrs. Rahimi's most effective approach would be to

    A. incorporate several choices of holiday-related topics into the planned writing activity.

    B. remind students of the importance of paying attention.

    C. allow students time to discuss the holiday and assign the writing activity for homework.

    D. postpone the writing activity until after the holiday and do an enrichment activity instead.

10. How can a teacher establish a positive climate in the classroom?

    A. Help students understand the unique contributions of individual differences.

    B. Divide students into groups by ability.

    C. Remove student choice from the teaching strategies used in the classroom.

    D. Use whole-group instruction for all content areas.

11. What is a good strategy for teaching an ethnically diverse class?

    A. Ignore the students' cultures.

    B. Imitate their speech patterns.

    C. Include ethnic studies and contributions in lessons.

    D. Expect them to accommodate your expectations for learning.

12. Two high school students are facing suspension for alleged violation of school rules. According to due process, the students have the right to which of the following?

    A. An informal hearing with a school administrator

    B. Makeup assignments to make up any missed work

    C. The right to have a lawyer present during questioning

    D. Placement in an alternative educational environment

13. In Mr. Hernandez's classroom, native English-speaking and native Spanish-speaking students are combined and encouraged to interact frequently. Mr. Hernandez monitors their interactions and tries to facilitate second language acquisition. This model is called

  A. acculturation.

  B. English-language development.

  C. dual immersion.

  D. transitional.

14. According to Piaget, what occurs during the developmental phase called equilibration?

  A. Schemata are proven inadequate to explain the environment.

  B. Responses to the environment are adjusted to agree with the schemata.

  C. Schemata are adjusted to agree with the environment.

  D. Schemata become adequate to explain the child's environment.

15. How many stages of intellectual development does Piaget define?

  A. 2

  B. 3

  C. 4

  D. 10

16. What would the presence of a short attention span and restlessness in a child be a possible indication of?

  A. Anger

  B. Dyspepsia

  C. Hyperkinesis

  D. Down's Syndrome

17. Who developed the theory of multiple intelligences?

  A. Bruner

  B. Dewey

  C. Gardner

  D. Freud

18. Research on short-term memory has suggested which of the following?

   A. The capacity is unlimited.

   B. Information must be rehearsed since it fades rapidly.

   C. It is easily retrieved.

   D. It is capable of in-depth processing.

19. On the Stanford-Binet test of intelligence, what is the average IQ score?

   A. 80

   B. 120

   C. 100

   D. 50

20. At approximately what age does a child begin to understand abstract concepts such as justice and democracy?

   A. 18–20

   B. 6–10

   C. 2–3

   D. 10–14

21. Which human motive is satisfied when teachers help students work toward challenging yet attainable goals?

   A. Achievement

   B. Influence

   C. Affiliation

   D. Clarification

22. Which of the following is NOT true about teacher planning?

   A. Most teacher planning is hidden from public view.

   B. Teacher planning is driven by the desire to make activities purposeful.

   C. A fair amount of teacher planning is a waste of time.

   D. Teacher planning makes up 10 to 20 percent of a teacher's work.

23. Which of the following seems to be a negative consequence of teacher planning?

    A. Teachers become less sensitive to students' ideas.

    B. Teachers become more sensitive to students' ideas.

    C. Teachers become less creative in their teaching.

    D. Teachers become less concerned with subject matter.

24. Teacher planning tends to eliminate

    A. student boredom.

    B. many management problems.

    C. student unrest.

    D. student failure.

25. According to Piaget, what stage is characterized by the ability to think abstractly and logically?

    A. Concrete Operational

    B. Pre-operational

    C. Formal Operations

    D. Operational

26. It is important to explain the goals and rationale for a lesson at its outset because

    A. students need to know what is expected of them.

    B. it establishes that the teacher is in control.

    C. it helps integrate new learning with prior knowledge.

    D. A and C are correct.

27. The direct instruction model helps students master

    A. problem solving.

    B. self-discipline.

    C. basic skills.

    D. conceptual information.

28. A practice common across most variations of cooperative learning is that student groups need to be heterogeneous. This practice is based, in part, on the principle that

   A. students should be separate but equal, as affirmed by *Brown v. Board of Education.*

   B. enhancing intergroup relations is more important than achievement.

   C. interethnic interaction promotes acceptance.

   D. experiential learning promotes reflection and efficacy.

29. According to research, what do children fear the most?

   A. Hunger

   B. Abandonment and loss of love

   C. Shameful situations

   D. Physical abuse

30. What do cooperative-learning methods all have in common?

   A. Philosophy

   B. Cooperative task/cooperative reward structures

   C. Student roles and communication

   D. Teacher roles

31. In a demographically homogeneous classroom, an issue that needs to be addressed is

   A. the unique needs of those who are different from "us."

   B. the contributions of our culture.

   C. that in a homogeneous population there are still unique differences of gender, socioeconomic status, and exceptionality, to name a few.

   D. that we need to help those who are less fortunate than we are.

32. In our diverse society, it is imperative that teachers

    A. teach all students to live in our society; if they can't speak the language, they need to learn to speak English. All students need to learn to be Americans.

    B. use teaching strategies that reach the majority of students.

    C. help families learn to act more American so that their children will appreciate the new culture and fit in better.

    D. analyze strategies for planning and adapting instruction that are responsive to the needs of all students to ensure that all students participate to the greatest extent possible in classroom activities.

33. Low SES (Socioeconomic Status), primary classrooms of effective teachers are characterized by

    A. no pauses between academic tasks.

    B. student choice in doing assigned tasks.

    C. cooperative-learning groups.

    D. more student-teacher interactions, less unengaged time.

34. When communicating with parents who don't speak English very well, or not at all, you should

    A. provide the same information you would to English-speaking parents and expect someone to translate it for them.

    B. provide materials whenever possible in their native language.

    C. not waste materials by sending them to people who can't read them.

    D. always use an interpreter for every communication.

35. What is an example of an academic transition or bridge signal?

    A. "Name the three simple machines."

    B. "That's the end of today's class."

    C. "That concludes our discussion of the first simple machine. Another simple machine is the incline plane; let's look at its characteristics now."

    D. "Today, we're going to discuss simple machines."

36. Which of the following statements is NOT recommended for teachers to use to check for student understanding?

    A. "Thumbs up if the statement I make is true."

    B. "Who would like to answer that question?"

    C. "Now, you all understand don't you?"

    D. "Raise your right hand if you think the answer to number four is. . . ."

37. One way to create a positive atmosphere in a classroom is to

    A. lead students to appreciate the value to the group of the differences among them.

    B. group students so that they are always taught with those of like abilities.

    C. teach all topics and subjects to everyone in exactly the same manner.

    D. seek to have a class whose population has very similar skills and abilities.

38. Over the summer, you learn that the ethnic mix of youngsters in your class this year will, for the first time, be very diversified. You can prepare for this new adventure by

    A. putting together all of the well-honed lessons that have worked for years.

    B. learning how to speak English with the same accent that will be used by a number of your students.

    C. planning projects that will include the ethnic contributions of the background of all of your incoming students.

    D. ignoring any differences. Everyone needs to be able to speak English to be successful in the United States.

39. Are all of the students basically the same in a homogeneously grouped classroom?

    A. Yes, all have the same ability level.

    B. Yes, all come from similar ethnic backgrounds.

    C. No, there are still unique differences to be found among the students.

    D. Yes, they have all had the same or similar life experiences.

40. In the United States we have a wonderful, and diverse grouping of peoples. Because of this, teachers need to

   A. help all of their students to melt into the mainstream of our society.

   B. be leaders for students who are trying to "Americanize" their parents.

   C. be sure that all of their students are aware of the laws of our country.

   D. plan instruction and activities that will be useful for all of their students so that all will be able to participate and profit from them.

41. Upon entering the classroom of a well-prepared teacher of students from disadvantaged neighborhoods, you would see

   A. a great number of activity choices for each student.

   B. strict discipline and absolute quiet.

   C. children in small groups working independently.

   D. frequent teacher-student interaction.

42. How can negative student behavior be best addressed in the classroom?

   A. Assign detention to the offender after berating him or her in front of peers.

   B. Use a consistent technique (such as Assertive Discipline's "name on the whiteboard technique"), so that the behavior does not interrupt the teaching.

   C. Send the offending student to the office for administrators to deal with.

   D. Stop the class and glare threateningly at the offender.

43. What is the most effective means of classroom management?

   A. Develop a reputation as a strict disciplinarian.

   B. Befriend students so they will like you and not act up in class.

   C. Create effective interactive learning so that students are engaged and motivated. Deal with negative behavior choices fairly and consistently.

   D. Keep a very stern demeanor until midterm.

44. Increasing student time-on-task behavior is closely related to

    A. adult, professional behavior on the part of the teacher.

    B. relying on whole-class instruction exclusively as instructional strategy.

    C. setting a specific time limit to accomplish a task.

    D. classroom silence.

45. Which arrangement of students in the classroom can help the development of cooperative learning in students?

    A. Learning groups or desks arranged so that students are clustered facing one another promotes cooperative learning and academic risk-taking.

    B. Desks arranged in rows encourage students to work together quietly.

    C. Desks arranged in a semicircle promote control.

    D. Flexible seating arrangements promote a friendlier classroom.

46. A way of effectively managing classroom behavior is to

    A. let students discipline their peers.

    B. ignore minor infractions of the rules.

    C. make behavior expectations clear and simple.

    D. use sarcasm and public ridicule to enforce classroom rules.

47. An effective teacher can use which of the following to communicate expectations to students?

    A. Tell the students what you expect them to do.

    B. Use a rubric.

    C. It isn't necessary to communicate expectations to students; they should know what you expect.

    D. Display graded student work around the classroom.

48. Which of the following is NOT an example of extrinsic motivation that can be used in a classroom?

   A. Offering added points to a test for answering a bonus question.

   B. Giving students homework-free passes for good performance on a test

   C. Giving praise for a good performance

   D. Expecting students to read a particular book because you explain to them how good it made you feel to read this book

49. How should teachers use rewards for good performance with students?

   A. They should be used sparingly.

   B. They should be used frequently.

   C. They should never be used.

   D. They should be used only with very bright students.

50. The use of immediate, positive feedback with students produces which results?

   A. Students' self-esteem is improved.

   B. Students answer more questions.

   C. Students perform better in cooperative learning situations.

   D. Students stay on task better.

51. Why is it important for teachers to determine students' prior knowledge before beginning a new topic?

   A. It allows prior knowledge to be incorporated in the teaching strategy as a bridge to understanding the new material.

   B. It gives a definitive starting point for the new material.

   C. It helps keep the new information organized.

   D. It allows the teacher to cover more content.

52. Sally is having difficulty preparing for tests in your class. She has failed two, despite "studying." What would you suggest for this third-grader as she prepares for the upcoming spelling test?

   A. Show her how to rehearse, using repetition. That is, have her repeat the word and its spelling 25 times.

   B. Berate her for not studying hard enough, and remind her if she fails she will be left back.

   C. Immediately recommend her for special education evaluation.

   D. Let her mother know that she is failing.

53. Your eighth-grade social studies class is an inclusion class with a wide variety of developmental and ability levels. How would you address the needs of all of your students?

   A. Teach to the middle of the class and use a bell curve to grade the students.

   B. Teach to the least able students and do not curve the grades.

   C. Use a variety of teaching strategies, and modify both instruction and evaluation based on the individual student.

   D. Modify only as required by IEP and hold all students to high standards.

54. José and Jorge are responsible students. José has an incomplete notebook and can't write a decent lab report in your tenth grade biology class. He does the experiments very well and, when questioned, gives excellent answers about what was done. Jorge has a fantastic notebook and perfect lab reports. However, his lab work is poorly done. What is your interpretation of this scenario?

   A. Jorge's parents must be doing his notebook and lab reports.

   B. José is just lazy.

   C. Both boys should be given extra work.

   D. José and Jorge have different intelligences and perhaps should be made lab partners.

55. What steps are important in the review of subject matter in the classroom?

    A. A rehearsal of the subject matter and a topic summary within the lesson

    B. A one-paragraph synopsis of the previous lesson and a review in writing at the end of the lesson

    C. A lesson preview, an in-depth discussion within the lesson, and a lesson-ending review

    D. A lesson-initiating review of prior lessons, the lesson topic, and a lesson-ending review

56. What is the best way to handle a student's incorrect response to a question?

    A. Have other students correct the response.

    B. Praise the student anyway and move on.

    C. Redirect the student to a better problem-solving approach.

    D. Respond with the word "wrong" and move to another student.

57. Billy has been caught stealing in your fifth-grade classroom. This has happened frequently before. What might be causing this behavior?

    A. Billy is emotionally disturbed.

    B. Billy needs the items he's stealing.

    C. Billy is in a normal stage of development.

    D. Billy is being taught to steal at home.

58. What is the most significant behavior developing in children between 18 months and 30 months of age?

    A. Socialization skills

    B. Language skills

    C. Potty training

    D. Identity

59. Kohlberg's theory of moral development is useful to classroom teachers as they examine expectations for their students' ability to

    A. behave appropriately toward their peers.

    B. perform on standardized tests of ability.

    C. use language appropriately.

    D. think abstractly.

60. Johnny's big brother was in your class last year, and you found him to be a poor student. Last year's teacher mentions in the faculty room that Johnny's parents are difficult to deal with.

    A.   You prepare for the worst and seat Johnny near your desk.

    B.   You immediately begin to dread Johnny being in your class.

    C.   You prepare to treat Johnny with high expectations and expect you will have a good year together.

    D.   You ask if Johnny can be transferred to someone else's class.

Directions: Constructed-Response questions are short essay questions that ask you to respond to a question indicating the grade level you are prepared to teach. Your response is scored on purpose, application of content knowledge and skill, and supporting evidence. It is not a test of your writing ability. Clarity is important. Be articulate and succinct, write legibly, in English, and focus on the topic of the question.

Constructed-Response Questions (Test Code 171)

1. *Student learning during the school year is influenced by many factors. Educators are likely to be most effective in working with their students when they understand how students learn and recognize specific factors that affect learning.*

    • *Identify a grade level for which you are prepared to teach;*

    • *Describe one classroom grouping practice that can be expected to influence student learning at the grade level you have identified; and*

    • *Explain two important ways in which the grouping practice you have identified is likely to affect student learning at that grade level.*

2. *Independent writing projects can be one of the most beneficial ways of conveying information to the students. They are also a good way of monitoring the students' understanding of topics they have encountered in their readings.*

    • *Identify a grade level you're prepared to teach.*

    • *List various writing projects that you could assign to your students.*

    • *Explain some of the benefits associated with each.*

Practice Test 1 (Code 171) Answer Key

Question	Answer	Competency
1.	B	3
2.	C	4
3.	D	3
4.	C	4
5.	D	4
6.	C	6
7.	C	5
8.	D	4
9.	A	4
10.	A	4
11.	C	3
12.	A	5
13.	C	3
14.	D	1
15.	C	1
16.	C	3
17.	C	1
18.	B	2
19.	C	1
20.	D	1
21.	A	4
22.	C	5
23.	A	5
24.	B	5
25.	C	1
26.	D	5
27.	C	4
28.	C	5
29.	B	1
30.	C	5

(Continued)

Question	Answer	Competency
31.	C	3
32.	D	3
33.	D	6
34.	B	3
35.	C	6
36.	C	6
37.	A	5
38.	C	3
39.	C	3
40.	D	3
41.	D	3
42.	B	5
43.	C	5
44.	A	5
45.	A	5
46.	C	5
47.	B	5
48.	D	6
49.	A	6
50.	D	6
51.	A	4
52.	A	2
53.	C	3
54.	D	2
55.	D	6
56.	C	6
57.	A	2
58.	B	2
59.	A	2
60.	C	6

Practice Test 1 (Code 171) Progress Chart

Competency 1

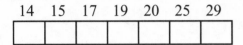

14	15	17	19	20	25	29

___/7

Competency 2

18	52	54	57	58	59

___/6

Competency 3

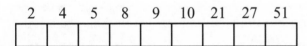

1	3	11	13	16	31	32	34	38	39	40	41	53

___/13

Competency 4

2	4	5	8	9	10	21	27	51

___/9

Competency 5

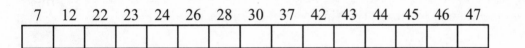

7	12	22	23	24	26	28	30	37	42	43	44	45	46	47

___/15

Competency 6

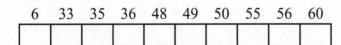

6	33	35	36	48	49	50	55	56	60

___/10

Detailed Explanations for Practice Test 1 (Code 171)

1. **B**

Students with access to few resources lack background knowledge and experience; hence, the genesis of the Federal Head Start Program.

2. **C**

Observation requires students to focus on specific features or elements of a skill in order to master it.

3. **D**

Immersion is a more effective strategy than exclusion for improved student acceptance and performance.

4. **C**

The design of the learning environment is an essential element in promoting student learning, and should be influenced, primarily, by the activities which the teacher plans to use.

5. **D**

Interdependence is fostered by relying on the members of a group for their individual areas of skill and excellence.

6. **C**

Using real-world examples and vivid descriptions communicates high expectations, which are an important element in student motivation.

7. **C**

For cooperative learning to be most effective in a classroom, and absorb the benefits of collaboration, acceptance, and varied learning styles, students need to be placed in groups by their complementary learning styles and varied intelligences.

8. **D**

Knowing what students should know and be able to do at the end of instruction is where all planning begins.

9. **A**

Developing an environment conducive to learning requires an understanding and accommodation of all external factors as they impact the instructional milieu.

10. **A**

A classroom climate where students feel valued and respected is achieved by teaching students to understand the unique contributions of individual differences. A family tree exercise often can help accomplish this.

11. **C**

A good strategy for teaching an ethnically diverse class can be seen in the answer above. By using multi-ethnic studies and the contributions of varied cultures students can come to understand the richness of varied and unique contributions to the American society.

12. **A**

For due process to be served in the educational environment, students have a right to a hearing before an impartial party.

13. **C**

Studies have indicated that immersion is the most effective strategy for integrating cultures and languages in a classroom.

14. **D**

According to Piaget, schemata are the integration of a student's realistic and experientially gained understanding of the way in which the natural world is organized.

15. **C**

The four stages are: Sensori-motor, Pre-operational, Concrete Operational, and Formal Operational.

16. **C**

Elements of ADHD (Attention Deficit Hyperactivity Disorder) are characterized by short attention span, restlessness, impulsivity, and acting-out behaviors.

17. **C**

Howard Gardner is the author of the highly regarded *Frames of Mind*, which introduced the concept of multiple intelligences.

18. **B**

Short-term memory has a lifespan of 30 seconds, unless it is an item of focus or rehearsed. Rehearsal takes the form of repetition or mnemonics, cues for memory retrieval.

19. **C**

The classic, although now largely discredited, Stanford Binet IQ test used 100 as its norm.

20. **D**

Piaget notes that it is during the Formal Operational stage (ages 10–14) that students begin to develop abstract concepts of justice and democracy.

21. **A**

The teacher's role as a constructor of learning involves the use of scaffolding, that process of supporting a student and then gradually removing the support. As scaffolding is removed and students become more independent, their sense of achievement is heightened.

22. **C**

Teacher planning is far from a waste of time. The practice of planning allows teachers to consider all of the elements in the learning environment so that learning can be effective. It eliminates wasted time, missing resources, and unworkable demonstrations that mar poorly planned experiences. Good planning ensures that students will "know and be able to do" at the end of a lesson.

23. **A**

Unless students are regularly consulted as to their needs, teachers end up planning in virtual isolation. Isolated creation of lessons makes teachers less flexible and less likely to consider student ideas "after the fact."

24. **B**

The primary tool for teachers in classroom management is effective and thorough planning of instruction, assessment, and the learning environment.

25. **C**

According to Piaget, adolescence is the stage in which students begin to develop abstract and logical thought. He called this final stage of human development: Formal Operational.

26. **D**

Teachers are most effective instructionally when they explain the goals and rationale of a lesson in the beginning of the lesson. It clarifies student expectations, allowing them to focus on what is expected of them, and it helps activate prior knowledge.

27. **C**

Direct instruction, often through lecture and note taking, is effective for the rapid dissemination of knowledge and basic skills. This is the base of Bloom's Taxonomy. Critical thinking skills require more sophisticated instructional strategies.

28. **C**

Interethnic interaction promotes acceptance. This concept is drawn from the highly successful immersion process. Its adaptation to cooperative learning is in the concept of students with varied gifts multiplying the outcome of a group.

29. **B**

Students fear abandonment and loss of love over physical pain, humiliation, hunger, or deprivation. This is a prime reason for the failure of the educational strategy of retention. Students experience that which they fear most when left behind by their peers, and they respond strongly emotionally.

30. **C**

For cooperative learning to be successful, students must be clear on the task, outcomes expected (communication), and their individual roles in the process.

31. **C**

Students need to be aware of the variety that exists even in homogeneous societies.

32. **D**

Though the majority culture often dominates our textbooks, instruction for diverse student populations needs to be responsive to all cultures and diversities, so that all children may participate.

33. **D**

The Coleman Report concluded that SES was a prime determinant of student performance. To break this cycle, students need to be personally engaged and challenged by the teacher, with little down time to become alienated, isolated, and uninvolved. Typically low SES students come to school with poor self-esteem and little educational experience.

34. **B**

When dealing with a diverse population, teachers are responsible for ensuring that parents are aware of educational and behavioral issues involving their children. For ESOL parents this may require translation of written information or the use of an interpreter for personal communication.

35. **C**

Teachers need to provide bridges between one concept and another. These bridges prevent students from falling behind. It carries them from one concept to another.

36. **C**

Checking for student understanding around a particular concept requires individual responses not universal acceptance.

37. **A**

Heterogeneous grouping decreases awareness of individual differences, perpetuates acceptance and collaboration, and creates a more positive classroom climate. Ability grouping, autocratic teaching methods, and a perpetual reliance on direct instruction causes students to be alienated from the group, aggressively competitive, and conceptually irrelevant — all negative indicators.

38. **C**

The process of inclusion, validation, and recognition stimulates student performance. This tends to counteract the isolating effects of diversity.

39. **C**

A guest lecturer from India, at a significantly non-diverse, suburban middle school, mentioned to the principal that she had never spoken to such a diverse population of students. Surprised, the principal questioned her as to this perception, and she noted that some students were blond, some redheads, some dark haired; some had blue eyes, some green. All of her students in India looked exactly like her.

40. **D**

Inclusion of all students in our educational process is a foundational principle of American public education.

41. **D**

In low SES classrooms at the primary level, student exposure to educational resources may be quite limited. Unengaged time, therefore, has little prior experience for filling it profitably.

42. **B**

Techniques such as "Assertive Discipline" are proven strategies for dealing with classroom management. They work because student expectations are clear. This allows students to make conscious choices based on known outcomes. In the absence of consistently understood consequences, students must continually probe to find their social boundaries.

43. **C**

Student awareness of social boundaries and consequences coupled with engaging, relevant, challenging instruction provides the necessary structure so that students can be successful. Reputation and respect stem from that.

44. **A**

Studies have clearly indicated a clear correlation between professional teacher behavior and students' time on task.

45. **A**

Cooperative learning as a teaching strategy is strongly correlated with academic risk-taking on the part of students. The physical classroom arrangement that is most conducive to consistent use of cooperative learning is the cluster or learning group.

46. **C**

Classroom management is based on clear, understandable expectations. Assertive discipline relies on fewer than seven rules in a classroom. Consistent application and clear expectations are the keys to effective classroom management.

47. **B**

A rubric is a matrix that explains teacher expectations for academic performance. When provided to students with a detailed explanation of the task, students can become independent learners.

48. **D**

Extrinsic motivation is an external reward for performance of a task. Although often associated with bribery, it is the first step in internalizing the motivation system. Giving students rewards is appropriate for high quality work, or a surprise benefit to work completed. They should be used sparingly or they become meaningless.

49. **A**

See explanation for question 48.

50. **D**

Immediate feedback is an extension of the reward system. It keeps students on task, and redirects their efforts when necessary.

51. **A**

Refer to the explanation for question 35. Developing bridges for student instruction requires an understanding of a student's prior knowledge.

52. **A**

As noted in the explanation for question 18, short-term memory lasts 30 seconds unless rehearsed. This is an effective way to address basic skills, but becomes less effective as the complexity of the concepts increases, and/or critical thinking is required.

53. **C**

A highly diverse classroom in any aspect requires an understanding and use of differentiated instructional strategies.

54. **D**

Awareness of the unique natures of our students allows us to address instruction to their strengths (Multiple Intelligence). Partnering students on a task blending their individual strengths is an effective means of addressing their instructional needs.

55. **D**

Effective instructional strategy requires activation of prior knowledge, the lesson, and a summative review.

56. **C**

Student questioning always puts students at academic risk when they respond. Careful management of the process makes students more willing to risk and to therefore learn rather than recite. Redirection, instead of a judgmental response, protects and encourages the students to take meaningful risks.

57. **A**

Lying, fighting, and stealing are not typical student behaviors. If the behavior is blatant and frequent, it is indicative of emotional distress. All chronic behaviors in young children need to be examined critically and addressed.

58. **B**

Psychologists agree that the acquisition of language skills in children around the age of two is the single most important developmental behavior in the human species. Persistent inability to orally communicate by the age of three is a significant hindrance to cognitive growth.

59. **A**

Kohlberg's theory of Moral Development proposes three levels: Pre-Conventional, Conventional, and Post-Conventional. As students negotiate these levels they become increasingly aware of behavioral expectations in society, and how to appropriately interact with their peers.

60. **C**

A student's perception of a teacher's expectations produces a self-fulfilling prophecy for the teacher in terms of those expectations.

Sample Responses to Constructed-Response Questions

Writing Samples with a Score of 3

1. I'm prepared to teach at the fourth-grade level. One grouping practice I would use in my classroom is small-group choral reading. I would separate the class into groups of 5-6 students, with each group including students who read at different levels. Using choral reading, the students in each group would read aloud together a grade-level reading selection (fiction or nonfiction). This grouping practice would allow all students a chance to read aloud regularly, which helps improve students' oral reading fluency, especially reading rate, voice inflection and intonation, and attention to punctuation. Choral reading in a small group is less threatening to students than reading aloud independently, so small-group choral reading would help promote fuller participation and greater comfort for many students. Also, unlike in a whole-class setting, by doing this activity in small groups, the weaker readers can hear the stronger readers more clearly, which provides them with a scaffold for improving their own performance by observing and following strategies used by the stronger readers. Meanwhile, the stronger readers would reinforce their own oral reading skills as well as their own self-confidence and motivation to continue improving. Finally, in a small group, the teacher can discern individual students' voices in order to monitor their progress, which helps inform future planning and instruction.

2. To monitor my 7th grade students' understanding of assigned reading topics, I could assign a research paper to them. The research paper will expand individual horizons with an understanding of new material, and/or offer a more personal, in-depth understanding of materials already covered by the course.

    Another form of independent student writing that I could assign to my students would be reviews (book, movie, play, music, newspaper, magazine, and/or journal articles). These writings would give my students a chance to interact with various forms of media while expanding their understanding of assigned topics.

    Additionally, and maybe more importantly, the review assignment will offer my students a chance to apply the theories that they acquired in the classroom to the external media, giving the students an opportunity to see classroom theory put into actual social practice.

    Finally, I could have my students keep daily and/or weekly reading journals, where each student can keep notes, ask questions and think abstract concepts through without regard for academic form or structure. I could then make periodic inspections of the students' journals to know what concepts need elaboration and what concepts are making sense.

Evaluation of Sample Responses

1. Purpose:

The writer addresses the question directly and immediately. She gives good evidence of experience in using her recommended strategy.

Application of Content Knowledge and Skills:

Her example of choral reading in a small group is well-documented.

Supporting Evidence:

The reasons given for the probable success of the teacher's planned strategy are logical and well described.

2. Purpose:

While this essay is a bit disjointed, the content addresses the advantages of each writing project and suggests how that project benefits not only the students but also the instructor. The essay follows the assignment by answering all parts of the question. It gives the impression that the writer is going somewhere with the idea because the writer has thought seriously about the topic.

Application of Content Knowledge and Skills:

The essay's main ideas are propelled by a succession of relevant supporting ideas, details, and examples.

Supporting Evidence:

The arguments are appropriate and clearly related to the ideas they support. Important words and ideas get clear emphasis and the word choices are accurate and appropriate to the context in which they are used. Thus, the question has been answered.

Practice Test 1

GACE Professional Pedagogy
(Code 172)

ANSWER SHEET FOR PRACTICE TEST 1 (CODE 172)

1. Ⓐ Ⓑ Ⓒ Ⓓ
2. Ⓐ Ⓑ Ⓒ Ⓓ
3. Ⓐ Ⓑ Ⓒ Ⓓ
4. Ⓐ Ⓑ Ⓒ Ⓓ
5. Ⓐ Ⓑ Ⓒ Ⓓ
6. Ⓐ Ⓑ Ⓒ Ⓓ
7. Ⓐ Ⓑ Ⓒ Ⓓ
8. Ⓐ Ⓑ Ⓒ Ⓓ
9. Ⓐ Ⓑ Ⓒ Ⓓ
10. Ⓐ Ⓑ Ⓒ Ⓓ
11 Ⓐ Ⓑ Ⓒ Ⓓ
12. Ⓐ Ⓑ Ⓒ Ⓓ
13. Ⓐ Ⓑ Ⓒ Ⓓ
14. Ⓐ Ⓑ Ⓒ Ⓓ
15. Ⓐ Ⓑ Ⓒ Ⓓ

16. Ⓐ Ⓑ Ⓒ Ⓓ
17. Ⓐ Ⓑ Ⓒ Ⓓ
18. Ⓐ Ⓑ Ⓒ Ⓓ
19. Ⓐ Ⓑ Ⓒ Ⓓ
20. Ⓐ Ⓑ Ⓒ Ⓓ
21. Ⓐ Ⓑ Ⓒ Ⓓ
22. Ⓐ Ⓑ Ⓒ Ⓓ
23. Ⓐ Ⓑ Ⓒ Ⓓ
24. Ⓐ Ⓑ Ⓒ Ⓓ
25. Ⓐ Ⓑ Ⓒ Ⓓ
26. Ⓐ Ⓑ Ⓒ Ⓓ
27. Ⓐ Ⓑ Ⓒ Ⓓ
28. Ⓐ Ⓑ Ⓒ Ⓓ
29. Ⓐ Ⓑ Ⓒ Ⓓ
30. Ⓐ Ⓑ Ⓒ Ⓓ

31. Ⓐ Ⓑ Ⓒ Ⓓ
32. Ⓐ Ⓑ Ⓒ Ⓓ
33. Ⓐ Ⓑ Ⓒ Ⓓ
34. Ⓐ Ⓑ Ⓒ Ⓓ
35. Ⓐ Ⓑ Ⓒ Ⓓ
36. Ⓐ Ⓑ Ⓒ Ⓓ
37. Ⓐ Ⓑ Ⓒ Ⓓ
38. Ⓐ Ⓑ Ⓒ Ⓓ
39. Ⓐ Ⓑ Ⓒ Ⓓ
40. Ⓐ Ⓑ Ⓒ Ⓓ
41. Ⓐ Ⓑ Ⓒ Ⓓ
42. Ⓐ Ⓑ Ⓒ Ⓓ
43. Ⓐ Ⓑ Ⓒ Ⓓ
44. Ⓐ Ⓑ Ⓒ Ⓓ
45. Ⓐ Ⓑ Ⓒ Ⓓ

46. Ⓐ Ⓑ Ⓒ Ⓓ
47. Ⓐ Ⓑ Ⓒ Ⓓ
48. Ⓐ Ⓑ Ⓒ Ⓓ
49. Ⓐ Ⓑ Ⓒ Ⓓ
50. Ⓐ Ⓑ Ⓒ Ⓓ
51. Ⓐ Ⓑ Ⓒ Ⓓ
52. Ⓐ Ⓑ Ⓒ Ⓓ
53. Ⓐ Ⓑ Ⓒ Ⓓ
54. Ⓐ Ⓑ Ⓒ Ⓓ
55. Ⓐ Ⓑ Ⓒ Ⓓ
56. Ⓐ Ⓑ Ⓒ Ⓓ
57. Ⓐ Ⓑ Ⓒ Ⓓ
58. Ⓐ Ⓑ Ⓒ Ⓓ
59. Ⓐ Ⓑ Ⓒ Ⓓ
60. Ⓐ Ⓑ Ⓒ Ⓓ

Practice Test 1 (Code 172)

Directions: Circle the best answer then mark it on your answer sheet.

1. A classroom teacher uses a variety of formal and informal methods to evaluate students' understanding in each instructional unit. The primary benefit to this strategy is that it is likely to

   A. help students develop an accurate perception of their own learning abilities.

   B. allow the teacher to monitor instructional effectiveness and make adjustments as needed.

   C. minimize students' anxiety levels with regard to testing.

   D. assure the teacher that she will have ample data for assigning a report card grade.

2. A high school teacher receives a phone call from the parents of one of his students who, they believe, he has disciplined unfairly. The teacher arranges a meeting, and to ensure effective communication during the meeting and a productive meeting overall, the teacher should begin the meeting with

   A. asking the parents what they feel would have been a more appropriate response.

   B. allowing the parents to express their views and emotions and to describe their understanding as to what occurred.

   C. reviewing the class and school rules with the parents.

   D. describing in detail the teachers' perspective of what occurred.

3. A first-year teacher asks her more experienced colleagues to observe in her classroom and give her constructive feedback. The benefit from this practice is that

   A. it makes the novice teacher more comfortable with the evaluation process.

   B. it will help the novice teacher learn to apply instructional practice more effectively in a real classroom context.

   C. it makes her more experienced colleagues like her more.

   D. it exposes the novice to diverse practices.

4. The No Child Left Behind Act

   A. increases funding for schools with low-achieving students.

   B. holds school districts accountable for their performance.

   C. increases the uses of the state testing programs.

   D. has no impact on handicapped students.

5. How may a teacher use a student's permanent record?

   A. To develop a better understanding of the needs of a student

   B. To help determine how she will seat her in the classroom

   C. To develop expectations for student performance early in the school year

   D. To record behavioral incidents for future reference

6. A teacher notices that a child has several bruises on his head and arms. When she asks about it, the child becomes angry and resentful, stating that he fell this morning. The teacher should

   A. wait and see if there are any other signs of abuse in the future before reporting this.

   B. talk to a more experience colleague for advice.

   C. forget about it; the child is probably just clumsy.

   D. report suspected abuse to the school counselor or administrator immediately.

7. You have heard a young teenage boy in your homeroom talking about suicide with other students. What do you do?

   A. Talk to the boy, and let him know you will be speaking to his parents about this incident.

   B. Report this immediately to the school psychologist.

   C. Report this immediately to your principal or assistant principal. Make your own report to authorities if required by school/district policy. Do nothing else.

   D. Ignore the incident; teenage boys are always looking for attention.

8. The No Child Left Behind Act requires all teachers to be

   A. highly qualified.

   B. highly professional.

   C. highly intelligent.

   D. highly educated.

9. You are a guest at a dinner party, and one of the other guests asks your opinion of the academic performance of their neighbor's son, who is in your class. You should

   A. explain what a good student the boy is, and how he could get into a good college with a bit more effort.

   B. politely explain that you do not discuss your students except with their parents and the student himself.

   C. leave the party immediately.

   D. tell an amusing anecdote concerning the boy in class.

10. A member of the board of education stops you on the street and, during the conversation, she complains about another teacher in your school. You should

    A. call the teacher immediately and warn him that the board of education is out to get him.

    B. inform your principal.

    C. stop the board member and politely suggest that this is not the appropriate place for this discussion; rather, it should be taken up with the board and the superintendent of schools.

    D. keep the conversation to yourself.

11. You have a workbook that students use in your classroom. Rather than order more copies and have less money in your budget for other things you wish to order, you

    A. make 30 copies for your class on the teachers copy machine and use the copies instead.

    B. tell your students not to write in the workbooks but to use a notebook for the answers.

    C. drop the workbook from your teaching strategy and use another technique or resource.

    D. make copies of the pages you use each day, until at the end of the year the students, in effect, have a complete workbook.

12. Innovations in assessment are partly a response to criticisms of the fairness and objectivity of standardized tests that have focused on all of the following EXCEPT

    A. class and gender bias.

    B. failure to measure students' general level of intelligence.

    C. failure to accurately measure students' skills.

    D. failure to measure students' levels of achievement.

13. The movement to assess student learning with ever-increasing number of tests has been brought on by

    A. declining test scores.

    B. international comparisons of student achievement.

    C. calls to hold teachers more accountable.

    D. all of the above.

14. When teachers measure students' attainment of knowledge and skills for the purpose of making decisions about their teaching, they are engaged in

    A. measurement.

    B. alternative assessment.

    C. formative evaluation.

    D. summative evaluation.

15. Most assessment approaches seek to answer the question, "Do students know content?" Performance-based assessment helps to answer what other important question?

    A. Do students commit information to memory efficiently?

    B. Can students reproduce what they know on tests?

    C. Are students capable of creative thought?

    D. How well can students use what they know?

16. Telling the story of a learner's growth in proficiency, long-term achievement, and significant accomplishments in a given academic area exemplifies the benefits of which assessment format?

    A. Portfolio assessment

    B. Performance-based assessment

    C. Formative assessment

    D. Pre-test evaluation

17. How does involving parents contribute to a productive learning environment?

    A. Productive learning environments are disorderly and do not focus on learning.

    B. Research has shown that when parents are involved, there is a contribution to a safe, orderly learning environment.

    C. Productive learning environments are primarily a factor between the student and the teacher and do not include the parents.

    D. Productive learning environments are a function of classroom management only.

18. Which of the following would be an effective strategy for a teacher to communicate with parents?

    A. Parent-teacher conferences

    B. Open houses and reports sent home

    C. Report cards and progress reports

    D. All of the above

19. According to the NCLB Act of 2001, schools that perform poorly over a six-year period

    A. could receive funds for student tutoring.

    B. may have a name change.

    C. could be bypassed for any type of funding.

    D. None of the above

20. Thelma Farquar is a new and nervous kindergarten teacher preparing for her first set of parent conferences. Among the tasks she needs to attend to is to

    A. set out comfortable chairs for parents across from her desk.

    B. put out fresh flowers and decorate the room.

    C. arrange side-by-side seating at a table.

    D. double-check her appointments.

21. A parent has left an angry message on a teacher's voice mail. The message relates to a concern about a student and is directed at the teacher. The teacher should

    A. call back immediately and confront the parent.

    B. cool off, plan what to discuss with the parent, then call back.

    C. question the student about what he said to the parent to cause the anger.

    D. ignore the whole thing.

22. What is the main responsibility of a mainstream classroom teacher to the special needs students in his classroom?

    A. To ensure that these students receive the special services and resources that they need.

    B. To let parents know of the disparity between these students and the rest of the class.

    C. To develop an IEP for the special-needs students.

    D. To provide the necessary special services for these students.

23. The superintendent of schools is required to

    A. supervise the senior teachers in the district.

    B. develop plans for school improvement.

    C. allocate the budget to the various schools in the district.

    D. implement plans and policies set by the board of education.

24. Which method of evaluation determines what students know and can do prior to or during instruction?

    A. Formative

    B. Summative

    C. Diagnostic

    D. Performance-based

25. The Individuals with Disabilities Education Act (IDEA) mandates that educational rights are to be granted to all people in what age category?

    A. Birth to age 21

    B. Three years of age to 21

    C. 6–18 years of age

    D. 6–21 years of age

26. Objective tests remain popular for all but which one of the following:

    A. Reliability is high.

    B. Objectivity is high.

    C. Electronic scoring is possible.

    D. Environmental complexity is high.

27. Tracking or ability grouping is acceptable in which one of the following situations:

    A. Interests or vocational aspirations

    B. Intelligence

    C. Ethnicity

    D. Tracking is never acceptable.

28. Site-based management is decentralized and has which of the following advantages?

    A. Teachers are highly involved but not highly accountable.

    B. Teachers are given decision-making authority.

    C. Administration assumes the role of decision maker with accountability.

    D. Administration is recognized as having the necessary expertise to guide outcomes.

29. Classroom environments should be structured to facilitate which of the following?

    A. Teacher control

    B. Student access

    C. Learning

    D. Student control

30. Which of the following is NOT an acceptable modification for special education students?

    A. Adjusting the size of assignments

    B. Varying the time allotments for assignments

    C. Decreasing the level of difficulty

    D. Assigning homework to introduce concepts

31. Teachers should base rules for the classroom on which one of the following factors:

    A. The rules children's parents have in their homes

    B. The developmental stage of the children

    C. What rules students in the classroom determine as a group

    D. What has traditionally been prescribed in schools

32. Which of the following explains why it is difficult for beginning teachers to establish consistency in enforcing classroom rules and procedures?

    A. Many beginning teachers do not believe in rules and procedures.

    B. Most rule breaking occurs when other things are going on.

    C. Most students do not respect beginning teachers.

    D. Most rule breaking occurs when the teacher is not in sight.

33. A question asking a student to name the capital of Brazil would be classified according to Bloom's Taxonomy as a(n)

    A. Knowledge question

    B. Application question

    C. Analysis question

    D. Evaluation question

34. Students who have an *external locus of control* exhibit which one of the following behaviors?

    A. Taking responsibility for their outcomes

    B. Experiencing pride for their success

    C. Giving credit for their accomplishments to others

    D. Attributing failure to lack of effort

35. How should a teacher respond to criticism from a colleague about his teaching?

    A. Criticize the criticizer.

    B. Dismiss the criticism as petty jealousy.

    C. Reflect on the criticism as objectively as possible; it might be true.

    D. Talk with other teachers to find out if she has criticized them as well.

36. Which of the following is a right of a parent or guardian?

    A. To be informed of a teacher's academic or social concerns about their child

    B. To have teachers use methods that the parents feel are best for teaching their child

    C. To constantly guide the teacher in the correct moral and social values to be used in the instruction of their child

    D. To be the sole administer of punishment when they believe their child requires it

37. The most useful definition of *curriculum* is which of the following?

    A. The academic offerings of the school.

    B. All the experiences in a child's life.

    C. The experiences, both planned and unplanned, that affect the education and growth of a child.

    D. All the educational experiences of a child, with the exception of extracurricula experiences.

38. Which of the following statements is NOT true of standards-based education and high-stakes tests based on those standards?

    A. A study of the Georgia assessment system found no evidence of teachers emphasizing whatever material they believed would raise test scores on the CRCT.

    B. Evidence suggests that elements of the curriculum not covered by these standards and tests are deemphasized.

    C. Teachers give priority to academic content covered by the tests.

    D. Evidence suggests that this approach encourages teachers to "teach to the test."

39. A performance standard specifies

    A. the condition under which students demonstrate knowledge.

    B. the audience for which standards are created.

    C. what students should know and be able to do.

    D. the terminal expectation of student learning.

40. An Interdisciplinary Instructional Unit

    A. is just a middle school thing.

    B. allows two or more teachers to develop several lesson plans with a common theme and joint outcomes.

    C. can be done only in a group or team approach.

    D. are confusing for students to follow.

41. In an era of standards-based instruction, teachers need to plan instruction

    A. that begins with an interesting activity.

    B. that is highly motivating for the entire class.

    C. that is in the teacher's greatest content strength.

    D. that is "backwards" from the standards.

42. When students use computers in school, they receive all of the following advantages EXCEPT

    A. enhanced social development.

    B. immediate feedback.

    C. increased motivation.

    D. essential twenty-first century skills.

43. What type of learning provides students with opportunities to inquire into subjects so that they discover knowledge for themselves?

    A. Mastery learning

    B. Inquiry learning

    C. Outcome-based learning

    D. Contingency learning

44. Scaffolding is based on the works of

    A. Vygotsky.

    B. Glasser.

    C. Greenberg.

    D. Cantor.

45. Research on cooperative learning suggests that

    A. it has a positive effect on the achievement of students with low levels of performance.

    B. students working together rarely develop positive attitudes about their classmates.

    C. students are best served by participating in few roles and responsibilities.

    D. this approach promotes racist attitudes.

46. Mr. Davis, a high school teacher, is chairperson of the curriculum development committee in math. His focus is on providing the facts, laws, and principles of math. He will most likely be advocating

    A. a student-centered curriculum.

    B. a college curriculum.

    C. a subject-centered curriculum.

    D. an integrated curriculum.

47. A mathematics teacher incorporates manipulatives into the lesson whenever possible. Which of the following will be the most likely result?

    A. Students will ignore the lesson and focus on playing with the manipulatives.

    B. Auditory learners will lose interest in math.

    C. Students will work together to achieve mastery of core concepts.

    D. Tactile learners will improve their understanding of mathematical concepts.

48. On the first day of class, a teacher allows students to sit wherever they like in the classroom. What will be the most likely result?

    A. Students will sit at random.

    B. Students will sit near their friends and be more likely to disrupt instruction.

    C. Students will pay more attention to instruction.

    D. Students will tend to come into conflict more often.

49. A second-grade teacher needs to introduce some difficult content-area knowledge to her class. Her students also need to go to lunch and have recess. Which of the following would be the ideal sequence for these activities?

    A. Recess, instruction, lunch

    B. Lunch, recess, instruction

    C. Recess, lunch, instruction

    D. Instruction, lunch, recess

50. Which of the following activities is most appropriate for teaching students about character development in a short story?

    A. Role play

    B. Constructing a diorama

    C. Class discussion

    D. Journal entry

51. A teacher is leading a mathematics unit when he notices that some students do not understand a prerequisite concept. How should the teacher handle this situation?

    A. He should continue with the new lesson.

    B. He should briefly review the earlier concept.

    C. He should stop the current lesson and do the prior lesson again in its entirety.

    D. He should try to incorporate the old lesson into the new one as much as possible.

52. Mr. Mahan, the physical education teacher, is working with the science, math, and family and consumer science (FACS) teachers to plan his unit on camping. Together they will be teaching performance standards in mapping, cooking, and tree identification. This is an example of

    A. inclusionary curriculum.

    B. student-centered curriculum.

    C. integrated curriculum.

    D. subject-centered curriculum.

53.   Research indicates that the effect of class size on achievement is

    A.   that low class size promotes higher achievement.

    B.   that high class size promotes high achievement.

    C.   that there is no clear relationship to class size and achievement.

    D.   the optimum class size is about twenty students per teacher, with achievement declining if the class size gets larger or smaller.

54.   In navigating the performance for grade exchange, students worry about two things

    A.   ambiguity and risk.

    B.   knowledge and affect.

    C.   beliefs and expectations.

    D.   critical thinking and group dynamics.

55.   A common, but erroneous, view held by many prospective teachers is that

    A.   teaching is like acting, and teachers need to be good performers.

    B.   teaching simply means telling students what they need to know.

    C.   most of their future students will be passive and unmotivated.

    D.   learning to teach requires a lifetime of hard work and reflection.

56.   For students, life in the classroom is different from the jobs they will hold in the future. This is because

    A.   work in school is mostly solitary, while jobs require much interaction with other people.

    B.   the workplace evaluates performance more harshly than schools.

    C.   technological tools are more common in schools than they are in the workplace.

    D.   schools do a better job of helping students meet their emotional needs than do typical workplaces.

57. The least restrictive environment refers to

    A. serving disabled students as much as possible in the regular classroom.

    B. establishing an individualized learning environment for disabled students.

    C. inclusion of disabled students in all school environments, like the library, cafeteria, etc.

    D. mainstreaming disabled students in regular school activities.

58. Where did most U.S. parents place blame for the problems currently facing public education in their communities?

    A. Lack of student motivation

    B. Societal problems

    C. Low school performance

    D. Poor teaching and teacher preparation

59. Historically, financial support for schools has come primarily from

    A. income tax.

    B. property tax.

    C. wage tax.

    D. tuition.

60. The basic unit of day-to-day school governance is

    A. the local school board.

    B. the town council.

    C. the PTA.

    D. the mayor.

Constructed-Response Questions (Test Code 172)

1. *You are a teacher planning instruction for students at a grade level you are prepared to teach. You are aware of the value of using various types of assessment to enhance instruction in your classroom.*

   - *Identify a grade level for which you are prepared to teach;*

   - *Describe one specific instructional situation at the grade level you have identified in which a selected-response test (e.g., multiple-choice, matching) would be an effective form of assessment; and*

   - *Explain one important reason why a selected-response test would be an effective form of assessment in the situation you have described.*

2. *You have noted that some of your students are not able to adequately read your subject text. You know that a content area textbook is often quite different from a typical reading textbook. You realize that even though you are a content area instructor, this does not excuse you from helping the students read a course text.*

   - *Identify your grade and subject area.*

   - *Describe some of the ways that the textbook for your course subject differs from a typical reading textbook.*

   - *Describe some ways that you can help a student improve his/her reading of your subject matter book.*

Practice Test 1 (Code 172) Answer Key

Question	Answer	Competency
1.	B	7
2.	B	10
3.	B	11
4.	B	7
5.	A	12
6.	D	12
7.	C	12
8.	A	10
9.	B	12
10.	C	12
11.	C	12
12.	B	7
13.	D	7
14.	C	7
15.	D	7
16.	A	7
17.	B	10
18.	D	10
19.	A	10
20.	C	10
21.	B	10
22.	A	9
23.	D	11
24.	A	7
25.	A	12
26.	D	7
27.	A	8
28.	B	11
29.	C	9
30.	D	8

31.	B	9
32.	B	8
33.	A	8
34.	C	8
35.	C	11
36.	A	12
37.	C	8
38.	A	8
39.	C	9
40.	B	9
41.	D	9
42.	A	9
43.	B	9
44.	A	9
45.	A	9
46.	C	8
47.	D	8
48.	B	8
49.	A	9
50.	A	8
51.	B	8
52.	C	8
53.	A	9
54.	A	8
55.	B	11
56.	A	8
57.	A	9
58.	B	10
59.	B	11
60.	A	11

Practice Test 1 (Code 172) Progress Chart

Competency 7

1	4	12	13	14	15	16	24	26

___/9

Competency 8

27	30	32	33	34	37	38	46	47	48	50	51	52	54	56

___/15

Competency 9

22	29	31	39	40	41	42	43	44	45	49	53	57

___/13

Competency 10

2	8	17	18	19	20	21	58

___/8

Competency 11

3	23	28	35	55	59	60

___/7

Competency 12

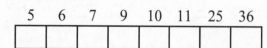

5	6	7	9	10	11	25	36

___/8

Detailed Explanations for Practice Test 1 (Code 172)

1. **B**

   Assessment informs instruction.

2. **B**

   To reach a level of cooperation and trust, parents and teachers must be aware of one another's perceptions of incidents and behaviors. Open communication is critical to the development of this trust.

3. **B**

   Effective feedback from critical friends in the real-world context of the classroom is important for professional growth of all teachers.

4. **B**

   The current iteration of NCLB holds school districts accountable for their performance. This unfunded mandate has a positive goal of providing equal educational opportunities for all students, it is however, deeply flawed as implemented.

5. **A**

   Confidentiality laws such as FERPA allow teachers to examine permanent records only if there is a demonstrable need to do so. A teacher's need to see these records is to better understand a student's educational needs and preferences. It is not an acceptable hunting ground for verification of behavioral concerns.

6. **D**

   A primary responsibility of classroom teachers is to exercise due care and diligence for her students. This involves ensuring the child's health and welfare. Suspected abuse must be reported immediately to the proper authority. (See your school policy.)

7. **C**

   Teachers act *in loco parentis* when children are with them in school. They have the same responsibility for due diligence and welfare as parents do for their own child during that time. Immediate and appropriate action must be taken to protect the health and safety of every child in the teacher's care.

8. **A**

   One characteristic of the NCLB was the requirement that every teacher be highly qualified—with no explanation of what that meant.

9. **B**

Federal laws and state code of conduct all require confidentiality on the part of teachers in regard to their students.

10. **C**

The authority of school board members is based on their service as part of the board. It does not extend to casual conversations. School board members are constrained by their code of conduct and FERPA laws in regard to personnel matters. The conversation can't be allowed to continue.

11. **C**

Copyright laws allow teachers to make one copy of materials for use in a classroom, or for research. They specifically prohibit any action that would damage market value of a product. Reproducing 30 copies of a workbook has an impact on market value and is therefore illegal.

12. **B**

The IQ test was so biased an instrument that it had no validity. Tests that claim to measure general intelligence have a problem with the definition of what general intelligence is.

13. **D**

The increasing number of mandated tests for students is an effort to understand and respond to declining test scores in traditional indicators such as the SAT and international assessments such as TIMS. Failure of our students to perform well on these measures has led to a cry for teacher accountability. This has neither been a popular nor highly successful approach.

14. **C**

There are two forms of assessment: formative and summative. Formative is that type of assessment that allows one to form opinions. It is an interim assessment to see if students and teachers are on the same train. A summative assessment captures what has been learned at the end of instruction.

15. **D**

The process called recitation (repeating what has been said to you) has dominated American education for 200 years. The 21st century requires more of students. Students must be able to actually apply what they have learned through a process called performance-based education.

16. **A**

A portfolio is a collection of student work that is specifically designed to demonstrate growth.

17. **B**

The research clearly shows parental involvement produces better schools and more productive students.

18. **D**

Parental involvement in schools requires frequent and effective home school communication. The advent of email has certainly improved this vital ingredient. The traditional means of parent conference, report cards, and progress reports (all now possible electronically) are still major factors in keeping this important communication link open.

19. **A**

Student performance and teachers' accountability for that performance is the backbone of the NCLB legislation. A still unfunded element of that legislation is tutoring.

20. **C**

During parent conferences, sitting with the parents rather than confronting them across a desk, establishes a feeling of cooperation and partnership instead of opposition.

21. **B**

Confrontations with parents are counter-productive. They are exhausting, unprofessional, and also negatively impact student performance and behavior. Always remain professional and under control of your emotions when dealing with parents.

22. **A**

The responsibility of the mainstream teacher to the special needs students in her class is to ensure that these students receive the special services and resources that they need. It is not to provide direct service. Other teachers and staff are specifically trained to provide those services, or to instruct the teacher as to how those services are to be delivered.

23. **D**

The superintendent is hired by the board of education (school board) to act as CEO of the school district. As chief executive officer his responsibilities do not include the supervision of lower level subordinates. Middle management performs that function.

24. **A**

See the explanation for question 14. Formative evaluation is done during or before instruction.

25. **A**

   IDEA was first authorized in 1975. It mandates educational rights to all students from birth to 21.

26. **D**

   Objective tests are popular because they are easily scored, they tend to be reliable, and objective. Environmental complexity is meaningless in this context.

27. **A**

   Ability grouping is frequently used and appropriate in the grouping of students around a particular skill.

28. **B**

   Site-based management is that configuration where the school site, and therefore the teachers, parents, and administrators, collaboratively make decisions affecting curriculum, hiring, resource allocation, and all other critical issues in the day-to-day operation of the school.

29. **C**

   The only reason for creating classroom environments in a variety of formats is to stimulate learning, based on the teacher's strategies.

30. **D**

   Special-needs students need a variety of interventions to create a level playing field in the classroom. Modifications of amounts of assignments, time, and degree of complexity are all appropriate. Expecting special needs students to teach themselves is inappropriate.

31. **B**

   The developmental level of the students in the class is the prime determinant on which classroom rules need to be based. Rules that are appropriate at the high school level are not functional at the elementary level.

32. **B**

   For new teachers, the problem with being consistent in enforcing classroom rules is that so many things occur in the dynamic of the classroom, that the novice is easily distracted.

33. **A**

   Bloom's Taxonomy includes the progression from knowledge to comprehension to synthesis to analysis to problem solving. The lowest level of the taxonomy is the fact type question, not the application of knowledge that follows.

34. **C**

These students, who have an external locus of control, attribute their accomplishments to others.

35. **C**

Criticism about one's teaching should always be considered, as it may be true.

36. **A**

The primary right of parents and guardians is to be informed of the social, academic, and behavioral performance of their children.

37. **C**

Curriculum can be defined as all the experiences both formal and informal, that affect the educational growth of a child.

38. **A**

Teachers in most Georgia public schools devote the entire month of March to the preparation of their students to take the CRCT. All districts have aligned the curriculum to the standards (GPS) and since the CRCT is aligned with the standards, the curriculum in most schools reflects what is tested on the CRCT.

39. **C**

Content standards specify what students need to know, performance standards specify what students should know and be able to do.

40. **B**

Interdisciplinary Instructional Units are the holistic approach to educational experiences for students. Instead of asking students to assemble disciplines into a complete conceptual understanding, an IIU assembles the concepts for students.

41. **D**

The focus on standards requires teachers to plan instruction from those standards, backwards. That is, what should students know and be able to do at the end of the unit, as a starting place.

42. **A**

Students using computers have little opportunity to interact with anything other than the computer. This does not enhance social skills, or understanding of diversity.

43. **B**

Inquiry or discovery learning is where students have the opportunity to explore activities and develop or "construct" their own learning.

44. **A**

Scaffolding is drawn from Vygotsky's work in that children require adult guidance through their zone of proximal development for cognitive growth to occur. That is, as students become more independent they require less adult guidance.

45. **A**

Cooperative learning has a positive affect on the achievement of all students, but especially on students with lower levels of performance. It allows their skills to be validated as significant in a group.

46. **C**

Subject or discipline centered teaching strategies focus on content to the exclusion of process. These strategies allow students to perform well on tests like the Georgia CRCT in the short run, but don't encourage application models.

47. **D**

There are a number of learning styles. Manipulatives work well for those who are tactile learners as opposed to auditory learners.

48. **B**

Planned classroom organization prevents mistakes in classroom management. It allows teachers to control their students' behavior, without overt techniques of discipline.

49. **A**

Placing the instructional experience between the non-structured periods allows the teacher to draw order from periods of relative rest.

50. **A**

Simulations are a practical and performance based method for teaching abstract concepts.

51. **B**

All students need to be kept on the same page. A brief review will bring the lost students up to speed, without wasting time of the students who are on target.

52. **C**

See explanation for question 40.

53. **A**

The correlation exists between lower class size and improved student achievement. There is no hard data on the actual number, just a range of between 10-25 students.

54. **A**

Students need an understanding of their expectations. Their greatest concerns are ambiguous requirements. They want to know what they need to do to be graded well. They are unwilling to take academic risks, for which they may be punished (graded poorly).

55. **B**

Teaching and learning are complex, sophisticated acts, that have dynamic requirements to be effective. It is no longer "teach, test, hope for the best."

56. **A**

Our schools often ignore Piaget's dictum that learning is a social activity. Schools focus on the solitary performance of individuals. The real world relies on collaboration and cooperation, skills not often emphasized in public schools.

57. **A**

IDEA requires students to be placed in the least restrictive environment, that is the environment where their needs can be met as close to or in the mainstream class as possible.

58. **B**

Most parents look at society and its concerns of violence, dishonesty, and sexual perversions as being responsible for the concerns faced in public schools.

59. **B**

Education is nationally supported by property taxes.

60. **A**

School boards are the elected officials who establish school policy.

Sample Responses to Constructed-Response Questions

Writing Samples with a Score of 3

1.   I am prepared to teach seventh-grade science. In a seventh-grade science class, I would use a selected-response (multiple-choice) test to evaluate my students' mastery of the facts, terminology, and other knowledge that has been covered in the classroom presentations and textbook readings for a particular unit of study. A unit typically contains a great deal of content. A selected-response format is especially useful for unit tests because this format allows the teacher to evaluate a broad sample of student learning from different sections and aspects of the unit. Each question can focus on a different fact, term, concept, or idea presented in the unit, and since students can answer multiple-choice questions quite rapidly, the teacher can ask many questions about many elements in the unit.

Limitations of selected-response tests often include difficulty in assessing students' ability to apply what they have learned and to use higher-order thinking skills, but well-written selected-response questions can sometimes overcome these limitations, as can including one or two essay questions on a mostly selected-response test.

Please note that the constructed-response answers don't have to be long. They have to be to the point, clear, legible, and answer the question asked.

2.   I am well aware that the history textbook to be used with my 8th grade class differs significantly from a typical reading textbook. Whereas a reading text often contains primarily narrative material, my history textbook contains chapters. The chapters include divisions and subdivisions; boldfaced words, maps, and diagrams (like timelines and population charts).

I intend to introduce the textbook by discussing with the students the use of headings and subheadings to set off the divisions of the chapters. I will also make sure that my students are able to read maps and that they watch for diagrams and boldfaced words.

Spending some time at the beginning of the school year to introduce the text to the students will be time that is well spent. I will also plan activities in which my students will be introduced to, and become familiar with, the specific language of history. With these preparations, my students will be able to use their book to their advantage, and this will save time for all of us in the long run.

Evaluation of Sample Responses:

1. Purpose:
The writer succinctly answers the question with valid reasoning for the use of multiple-choice questions on seventh grade science tests.

Application of Content Knowledge and Skills:
The writer chooses the setting of a science class to highlight the particular needs of such a class. She uses this information to validate the use of multiple-choice questions.

Supporting Evidence:
Well-reasoned arguments are extended for the use of such questions in this arena.

2. Purpose:
The well-structured essay answers all the questions. This subject matter teacher will present students with ideas on how to read the content area material effectively. A good subject matter teacher helps the students read the content area material.

Application of Content Knowledge and Skills:
The answer is professional and offers good advice to the teacher of the content areas.

Supporting Evidence:
By introducing the textbook to the class and discussing the skills needed in reading the text, the teacher can improve the skills of the students, and make her/his work easier.

Practice Test 2

GACE Professional Pedagogy (Code 171)

ANSWER SHEET FOR PRACTICE TEST 2 (CODE 171)

1. Ⓐ Ⓑ Ⓒ Ⓓ   16. Ⓐ Ⓑ Ⓒ Ⓓ   31. Ⓐ Ⓑ Ⓒ Ⓓ   46. Ⓐ Ⓑ Ⓒ Ⓓ

2. Ⓐ Ⓑ Ⓒ Ⓓ   17. Ⓐ Ⓑ Ⓒ Ⓓ   32. Ⓐ Ⓑ Ⓒ Ⓓ   47. Ⓐ Ⓑ Ⓒ Ⓓ

3. Ⓐ Ⓑ Ⓒ Ⓓ   18. Ⓐ Ⓑ Ⓒ Ⓓ   33. Ⓐ Ⓑ Ⓒ Ⓓ   48. Ⓐ Ⓑ Ⓒ Ⓓ

4. Ⓐ Ⓑ Ⓒ Ⓓ   19. Ⓐ Ⓑ Ⓒ Ⓓ   34. Ⓐ Ⓑ Ⓒ Ⓓ   49. Ⓐ Ⓑ Ⓒ Ⓓ

5. Ⓐ Ⓑ Ⓒ Ⓓ   20. Ⓐ Ⓑ Ⓒ Ⓓ   35. Ⓐ Ⓑ Ⓒ Ⓓ   50. Ⓐ Ⓑ Ⓒ Ⓓ

6. Ⓐ Ⓑ Ⓒ Ⓓ   21. Ⓐ Ⓑ Ⓒ Ⓓ   36. Ⓐ Ⓑ Ⓒ Ⓓ   51. Ⓐ Ⓑ Ⓒ Ⓓ

7. Ⓐ Ⓑ Ⓒ Ⓓ   22. Ⓐ Ⓑ Ⓒ Ⓓ   37. Ⓐ Ⓑ Ⓒ Ⓓ   52. Ⓐ Ⓑ Ⓒ Ⓓ

8. Ⓐ Ⓑ Ⓒ Ⓓ   23. Ⓐ Ⓑ Ⓒ Ⓓ   38. Ⓐ Ⓑ Ⓒ Ⓓ   53. Ⓐ Ⓑ Ⓒ Ⓓ

9. Ⓐ Ⓑ Ⓒ Ⓓ   24. Ⓐ Ⓑ Ⓒ Ⓓ   39. Ⓐ Ⓑ Ⓒ Ⓓ   54. Ⓐ Ⓑ Ⓒ Ⓓ

10. Ⓐ Ⓑ Ⓒ Ⓓ   25. Ⓐ Ⓑ Ⓒ Ⓓ   40. Ⓐ Ⓑ Ⓒ Ⓓ   55. Ⓐ Ⓑ Ⓒ Ⓓ

11. Ⓐ Ⓑ Ⓒ Ⓓ   26. Ⓐ Ⓑ Ⓒ Ⓓ   41. Ⓐ Ⓑ Ⓒ Ⓓ   56. Ⓐ Ⓑ Ⓒ Ⓓ

12. Ⓐ Ⓑ Ⓒ Ⓓ   27. Ⓐ Ⓑ Ⓒ Ⓓ   42. Ⓐ Ⓑ Ⓒ Ⓓ   57. Ⓐ Ⓑ Ⓒ Ⓓ

13. Ⓐ Ⓑ Ⓒ Ⓓ   28. Ⓐ Ⓑ Ⓒ Ⓓ   43. Ⓐ Ⓑ Ⓒ Ⓓ   58. Ⓐ Ⓑ Ⓒ Ⓓ

14. Ⓐ Ⓑ Ⓒ Ⓓ   29. Ⓐ Ⓑ Ⓒ Ⓓ   44. Ⓐ Ⓑ Ⓒ Ⓓ   59. Ⓐ Ⓑ Ⓒ Ⓓ

15. Ⓐ Ⓑ Ⓒ Ⓓ   30. Ⓐ Ⓑ Ⓒ Ⓓ   45. Ⓐ Ⓑ Ⓒ Ⓓ   60. Ⓐ Ⓑ Ⓒ Ⓓ

Practice Test 2 (Code 171)

1. What stage of development did Piaget characterize as having the ability to think abstractly?

   A. Pre-operational

   B. Formal operational

   C. Concrete operation

   D. Post-operational

2. Kohlberg's Moral Development Theory notes that the level of development in which decisions are made based on physical consequences are

   A. pre-conventional level.

   B. post-conventional level.

   C. parental fear level.

   D. symbolic level.

3. Which of the following is a belief of cognitive psychologists?

   A. By changing environmental conditions, one can control student behavior.

   B. All people pass through developmental stages, although at varying rates.

   C. Learning involves constructing individual knowledge from individual experiences.

   D. Responses are influences by the consequences that follow them.

4. Extrinsic reinforcement can be usefully employed in all but which of the following cases?

   A. Involving students in a boring task

   B. Providing feedback for positive progress

   C. Building self-esteem

   D. Increasing interest in a task

5.   Behaviorists believe which of the following?

    A.   Students learn by observing models.

    B.   Behavior can be controlled by manipulating the environment.

    C.   Students construct their own reality.

    D.   Punishment has little effect on student behavior.

6.   The effective teacher selects learning activities that

    A.   are based on specific learning objectives.

    B.   are in accord with the teacher's specific area of interest and expertise.

    C.   are in the textbook.

    D.   are highly motivating.

7.   State or national standards drive the curriculum in most schools. Standards are organized into scope and sequence. What is scope?

    A.   The repetition of the content

    B.   The depth of the content

    C.   The span of the curriculum

    D.   Instructional objectives

8.   Learning activities for younger students need to focus on short time frames in simplified form because

    A.   with TV students are easily bored.

    B.   their brains aren't fully developed yet.

    C.   their parents will be helping with the homework and if it's too complex they wouldn't be able to follow it.

    D.   the students' attention span is approximately their age plus one minute.

9.   As students pass through different levels of development (Emotional, Linguistic, physical, Cognitive, and social), as a teacher, it is important to remember that

    A.   it is just a stage and that it will pass.

    B.   the stages are intricately related; they are not exclusive.

    C.   the stages are exclusive.

    D.   learning is only involved with the cognitive development of a child.

10. Direct instruction is used in the classroom as

    A.   the best means to control and teach kids.

    B.   the quickest way to transfer knowledge in the classroom.

    C.   the way to increase attention span.

    D.   an appeal to all of the multiple intelligences.

11. Whole group instruction is used by a classroom teacher most effectively when

    A.   discussing an assignment.

    B.   when you want full class participation.

    C.   when peer based learning is not an issue.

    D.   when the topic is covered in the textbook.

12. Maslow's Hierarchy of Needs suggests which scenario would most likely impair a student's ability to concentrate in the classroom?

    A.   A poor degree of self-actualization

    B.   An undeveloped aesthetic appreciation

    C.   Alienation from peers

    D.   Poor test results on a single test

13. What must be a consideration when a parent tells a teacher that the parent is at her wit's end because she just can't control her child?

    A.   Should the parent take parenting classes?

    B.   Should the child be threatened by the teacher?

    C.   Consider whether the parent's expectations for control are developmentally appropriate.

    D.   Consider whether the parent's rules are too rigid.

14. Why is Kohlberg's Theory of Moral Development important to classroom teachers?

    A.   It explains language acquisition.

    B.   It explains logical thought acquisition.

    C.   It explains the stages of moral development of a child.

    D.   It explains the psychosocial development of a child.

15. Howard Gardner's Theory of Multiple Intelligence allows educators to

    A. design learning methods and environments in their classrooms to maximize student learning.

    B. help students to become better auditory learners.

    C. explain to parents why a student is failing algebra.

    D. create better lectures.

16. Constructivism is that theory of learning that

    A. indicates learning is developmental.

    B. was developed by Piaget.

    C. indicates that the learner creates knowledge.

    D. is useless in today's environment of No Child Left Behind.

17. To a classroom teacher, diversity can be defined as

    A. racial differences only.

    B. ethnic and minority concerns in a classroom only.

    C. differences among learners, classroom settings, and academic outcomes.

    D. not an important concern in creating classroom strategies.

18. In Mrs. Rahimi's 6th grade classroom, the student population is highly diverse. She needs to plan her lessons

    A. with sensitivity for that diversity in her use of cultural and diverse resources in her curriculum and instructional practices.

    B. using common practices for all students so they fit into the majority culture.

    C. ignoring the diversity and treating every student fairly and equally.

    D. and then ask for a classroom with greater homogeneity.

19. In developing teaching strategies, Mrs. Rahimi should focus on

    A. making sure all material is covered.

    B. trying to keep pace with other teachers of 6th grade students in her school.

    C. making sure she challenges her brightest students.

    D. developing strategies that ensure all students reach proficiency.

20. If an educational program is child-centered, it will

    A.   be taught by specially trained teachers.

    B.   take its cues from student interests, abilities, and needs.

    C.   be taught in a circle.

    D.   not be developed by the teacher, rather it will be created by
         the students.

21. As Mrs. Rahimi begins addressing critical thinking skills with her students, she
    looks to everyday activities that require these skills such as

    A.   taking multiple-choice tests.

    B.   bringing homework to class completed and correct.

    C.   showing up on time for school.

    D.   gathering information from a diversity of sources to complete
         a project.

22. Which of the following best describes the relationship between teachers'
    expectations and student learning?

    A.   It is inverse, as expectations go up, learning goes down.

    B.   It is direct, as expectations go up, learning goes up.

    C.   It is complex, sometimes inverse, sometimes direct.

    D.   There is no relationship.

23. In developing appropriate strategies for teaching her third-grade class, Ms. Dailey
    looked to the in-school resources of the library and media center and found them
    underfunded and poorly supplied. Her next direction might well be

    A.   clubs, societies, and civic organizations in her community.

    B.   complaining to the school committee.

    C.   spending her own money.

    D.   making her students earn the money by selling magazines
         door-to-door.

24. Johnny has been acting strangely in your 10th grade home economics class lately. In finding answers to this concern, you should contact any of the following EXCEPT

    A. the guidance counselor.

    B. other teachers who have John in class.

    C. his mother.

    D. the State Social Service Agency.

25. Symptoms of attention deficit disorder (ADD) include which of the following?

    A. Learning disabilities and below average IQ

    B. Below-average IQ and problems awaiting turns

    C. Reclusiveness and learning disabilities

    D. Problems awaiting turns and impulsiveness

26. How can student misconduct be redirected at times?

    A. Threatening the student

    B. Whole class punishment

    C. Glaring at the disruptive student

    D. Moving closer to the student (proximal) while continuing to teach

27. Which of the following will significantly increase appropriate student behavior in the classroom?

    A. A stern demeanor

    B. Contacting parents at the first sign of misbehavior

    C. Having class rules that are consistently enforced in a fair and impartial manner, with clear and appropriate consequences

    D. Having class rules and giving feedback

28. Mrs. Devine has reached her limit and becomes extremely angry with behavior in the classroom. She stops instruction and yells at the students for five minutes to the point where she is exhausted, red in the face, and near tears. This is likely to cause the students to

   A.   feel guilty and stop all misbehavior.

   B.   respond with more behavior disruption.

   C.   ignore the whole incident and continue as if nothing had happened.

   D.   run screaming from the room.

29. What is the nature of effective praise?

   A.   It is given frequently.

   B.   It is given only in extreme cases.

   C.   It is in writing.

   D.   It is specific about the particulars of the achievement.

30. Mrs. Jackson gives frequent oral praise in her class. How might she supplement this to be even more effective?

   A.   Help students to evaluate their own performance and teach them to self-reinforce.

   B.   Give candy or stickers to reinforce.

   C.   Have students give one another praise by clapping.

   D.   Give fewer instances of verbal praise.

31. Mr. Davis introduced a new geography lesson to his fifth graders. He tells them that the new project will be very challenging, but he knows that all of the groups will do a great job. This is an example of

   A.   time on task.

   B.   high expectations.

   C.   clear rules and procedures.

   D.   feedback.

32. Mr. Davis has developed a lesson using the following parts: daily review, presentation, guided practice, corrective feedback, independent practice, and weekly and monthly reviews. What type of instructional model does this represent?

    A. Constructivist

    B. Product-process

    C. Direct instruction

    D. Cooperative learning

33. Which of the following teacher actions would work best with at-risk students?

    A. Active teaching in whole class settings

    B. Fragmentation of concepts into small easily understood bits

    C. Avoid complex issues, ask recall type questions frequently

    D. Emphasize major concepts and big ideas rather than basic skills

34. Which of the following is NOT a necessary professional knowledge base for teachers?

    A. Knowledge of government and society

    B. Knowledge of learners and educational aims

    C. General pedagogical knowledge

    D. Pedagogical content knowledge

35. Which of the following adjectives characterize an ineffective teacher?

    A. Alert, poised, democratic, and confident

    B. Understanding, warm, steady, and responsive

    C. Kind, attractive, fair, and authoritarian

    D. Alert, warm, fair, and kind

36.   Why is it important for teachers to be reflective about their practice?

    A.   There is a sound knowledge base on teaching, and reflection helps teachers to master it.

    B.   Traditional practices offer solutions to most problems facing teachers; reflection helps teachers acquire these practices.

    C.   Teaching presents teachers with unique situations; reflection helps to find the best solution to these situations.

    D.   Most teaching problems don't have answers; reflection allows one to continue despite this point.

37.   Which of the following statements most accurately reflects what research tells us about the teacher's impact on student achievement?

    A.   Teachers have a very strong influence on student achievement.

    B.   Teachers don't have a strong influence on student achievement.

    C.   Early studies indicated that teachers did not have much impact on student achievement; these findings were later proved inaccurate.

    D.   The Coleman Report indicates that SES is the sole determinant of student achievement.

38.   One way many teachers can prevent many discipline problems is to

    A.   thoroughly plan rules and procedures.

    B.   carefully arrange the classroom layout and décor.

    C.   thoughtfully prepare interesting and appropriate instruction.

    D.   do all of the above.

39.   Anna was sidetalking, and her teacher, Ms. Logan, moved to stand by her as she was giving directions for her next activity. Ms. Logan's actions are an example of

    A.   proximity control.

    B.   logical consequences.

    C.   assertive discipline.

    D.   attention getting.

40. Which factor limits the validity of tests?

    A. Parental interference

    B. Administrative errors

    C. Student fatigue

    D. Curriculum integration

41. A mastery orientation to motivation is best defined as

    A. a focus on affirming one's self-worth by competing with and beating others.

    B. a belief that effort is linked to learning and that learning is inherently satisfying.

    C. a desire to have input into decisions that affect your learning.

    D. a high academic self-concept.

42. Some element of cooperative learning is in all of the following EXCEPT

    A. positive interdependence.

    B. face-to-face interaction.

    C. individual accountability.

    D. individual work.

43. Mrs. Grey is a second grade teacher who wants to clearly express the rules of the class to her students. She wants rules that are consistent with self regulated learning and classroom democracy. Which of the following rules best meets Mrs. Grey's goals?

    A. Always raise your hand before speaking in class.

    B. Students who forget their homework will not be allowed to have recess.

    C. Always put forth your best effort.

    D. No gum chewing in class.

44. In his health class Mr. Mahan says that the immune system is like a country's system of military defense. Certain parts act like forts, some like scouts, some like weapons. This is an example of

   A.   advance organizer.

   B.   summative organizer.

   C.   research organizer.

   D.   simile organizer.

45. Ms. Lockamy is interested in improving her students' performance. After reviewing several video tapes of her classes, she finds she usually waits 2 seconds for students to respond to her questions and 3 seconds to respond to their answers. She should consider

   A.   increasing the wait time given for students to answer her questions.

   B.   slowing down.

   C.   decreasing the wait time given to students to answer questions.

   D.   listening more and talking less.

46. The following are all forms of cooperative learning EXCEPT

   A.   pair share.

   B.   three step interview.

   C.   true-false test.

   D.   jigsaw.

47. To begin a behavior self-management program with your students, you need to do all of the following EXCEPT

   A.   choose just one behavior to begin focusing on.

   B.   expect students to know how to monitor their behavior on their own to start with.

   C.   when the first behavior issue shows improvement introduce a second behavior.

   D.   define the exact behavior to be monitored for the student.

48. Which of the following is NOT an example of authentic assessment?

    A. Writing a travel brochure about your town

    B. Making a map of your town

    C. Writing the formula for the area of a rectangle on a test

    D. Producing a video about your town

49. As a new teacher it is imperative to be aware of the following when teaching in a culturally diverse classroom EXCEPT

    A. your student's value systems.

    B. sensitivity for the student's families and lifestyles.

    C. relevance of the curriculum to the culture of the students.

    D. need for the students to adapt to the cultural and behavioral standards of the majority population.

50. The U.S. Department of Education released a report in 2002 that the total percent of students enrolled in special education in the United States was

    A. 5%.

    B. 50%.

    C. 25%.

    D. 12%.

51. The following are all considered to be learning disabilities and are addressed under PL 94-142, EXCEPT

    A. dyslexia.

    B. dyspepsia.

    C. dyscalculia.

    D. dyspraxia.

52. Teachers must understand that learning disabilities affect students

    A. from single parent families primarily.

    B. with low IQ's.

    C. who may have an average to above average intelligence.

    D. from poverty.

53. As a new teacher, Quentin Farquar knew that classroom management was a critical element in his effectiveness during his first year. He carefully reviewed what he knew about effective strategies for establishing an organized and productive learning environment. Mr. Farquar knew that in implementing effective classroom routines

    A. he would have to give punishment assignments regularly.

    B. it will be easier for his students to cope with changes and distractions that will occur throughout the school year.

    C. nothing can ever be allowed to interrupt the classroom routine.

    D. his students will have difficulty with change, but he would be more in control in his classroom.

54. Mr. Farquar has many things to consider as he develops his classroom management plan. The routines and procedures that he should consider include all of the following EXCEPT

    A. "How many items should he include as procedures?"

    B. "Which items are most important?"

    C. "Do his procedures have the approval of the students' parents?"

    D. "Are they appropriate requirements for the grade/developmental level of his students?"

55. The American Indian community has a very high dropout rate from the U.S. public school system. One possible reason for this may be that

    A. there is a high rate of poverty.

    B. parents are overly involved in the school system.

    C. they are conformists.

    D. they disagree with the disciplinary measures enforced in many schools.

56. In the diverse cultures found in American public school classrooms the needs of the diverse populations include all of the following EXCEPT

    A. inclusion.

    B. respect.

    C. understanding.

    D. concessions.

57. When developing routines for use in the classroom, it is important to remember that

    A. the routines must be appropriate and applicable to the students themselves; students at different levels will have vastly different needs.

    B. some basic routines are consistent and can be applied at all levels.

    C. students thrive on change and routines are too confining.

    D. routines need to be consistent across all levels.

58. Ms. Logan is getting ready for her first assignment as a seventh grade language arts teacher. As she creates classroom procedures, she remembers to

    A. cover every concern that she has heard about or seen in her limited experience.

    B. spend time with her mentor to make sure every possibility has been addressed.

    C. not overwhelm her students with too many procedures.

    D. introduce all procedures on the first day.

59. Mr. Davis is expected to use differentiated instruction in his class given their varied abilities and skill levels. To do this Mr. Davis will

    A. give all students the same assignment; wait for everyone to finish before moving to the next concept.

    B. set up different assignments for different student levels, sort of like a band director.

    C. require that all assignments be completed in a set amount of time.

    D. teach, test, and hope for the best.

60. As a new classroom teacher, a major concern is classroom management. It is important to remember to do all of the following EXCEPT

    A. plan and manage instructional techniques prior to teaching.

    B. help students develop a sense of fairness and respect.

    C. communicate and model appropriate behavior.

    D. create sufficiently severe punishments to deter negative classroom behavior.

Constructed-Response Questions (Test Code 171)

1. *Address the following with the subject area and grade level you are prepared to teach.*

   - *Why is it important for teachers to focus on having their students learn Critical Thinking Skills or Habits of the Mind rather than on learning just content?*

   - *Describe two strategies to help students meet this goal (learning critical thinking).*

   - *Explain why this would be an effective strategy.*

2. *Every teacher must, at some time or another, deal with an intentionally disruptive student. While each student and situation will be different, there are still certain fundamental approaches to dealing with disruptive students.*

   - *Identify a grade level for which you are prepared to teach.*

   - *Name two approaches you could use in dealing with disruptive students.*

   - *Describe how you would implement them.*

Practice Test 2 (Code 171) Answer Key

Question	Answer	Competency
1.	B	1
2.	A	1
3.	C	1
4.	D	6
5.	B	1
6.	A	1
7.	C	1
8.	D	1
9.	B	1
10.	B	1
11.	A	1
12.	C	1
13.	C	1
14.	C	1
15.	A	2
16.	C	2
17.	C	3
18.	A	3
19.	D	2
20.	B	3
21.	D	2
22.	B	3
23.	A	3
24.	D	3
25.	D	3
26.	D	4
27.	C	4
28.	B	4
29.	D	4
30.	A	4

31.	B	5
32.	C	5
33.	D	5
34.	A	5
35.	C	5
36.	C	5
37.	A	5
38.	D	5
39.	A	5
40.	C	5
41.	B	6
42.	D	5
43.	C	6
44.	A	6
45.	A	6
46.	C	5
47.	B	5
48.	C	3
49.	D	3
50.	D	3
51.	B	3
52.	C	3
53.	B	5
54.	C	5
55.	A	3
56.	D	4
57.	A	5
58.	C	5
59.	B	5
60.	D	5

Practice Test 2 (Code 171) Progress Chart

Competency 1

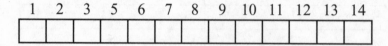

__/13

Competency 2

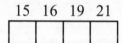

__/4

Competency 3

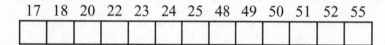

__/13

Competency 4

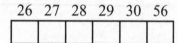

__/6

Competency 5

31 32 33 34 35 36 37 38 39 40 42 46 47 53 54 57 58 59 60

__/19

Competency 6

__/5

Detailed Explanations for Practice Test 2 (Code 171)

1. **B**

Ideological issues and abstract thinking, such as concerns about the future, are characteristics of this stage.

2. **A**

Decisions that are based on physical consequences are pre-conventional.

3. **C**

Cognitive classifies children's psychological development into stages based on their age and individual experience.

4. **D**

Increasing interest in a task isn't an extrinsic reinforcement.

5. **B**

Having a behavior reinforced by someone, other than the student, to shape or control what is learned.

6. **A**

Learning activities should reflect the learning objectives.

7. **C**

The activity or subject area covered within a curriculum defines scope.

8. **D**

Because young children have difficulty taking on the viewpoints held by others, lessons should be simplified.

9. **B**

Human development is a cumulative result of life experiences.

10. **B**

If time is limited, direct instruction is used because it is the quickest way to transfer knowledge.

11. **A**

Whole group instruction is the most efficient method to use when discussing an assignment.

12. **C**

A student's ability to concentrate in the classroom is influenced by the environment.

13. **C**

A parent's expectations for control should be developmentally appropriate to the child's age.

14. **C**

Kohlberg's theory explains the stages of moral development of a child.

15. **A**

We can use Gardner's theory as a foundation for creating lessons that will appeal to all types of learners.

16. **C**

Constructivism is a process in which students build new knowledge on top of existing knowledge.

17. **C**

Diversity is the multiple differences among learners in a classroom setting.

18. **A**

Curriculum instructional practices should reflect the characteristics of a diverse student population.

19. **D**

Teaching strategies must be analyzed in order to ensure that all students reach proficiency.

20. **B**

Students learn best in programs that are sensitive to their needs and in which their capabilities are understood.

21. **D**

Higher-level skills, such as critical and creative thinking and problem solving, are enriched in this process.

22. **B**

We can build student confidence and foster a desire to learn when we show that we have expectations of them.

23. **A**

Outside resources are often necessary for school systems to receive supplies that are needed.

24. **D**

Show sensitivity for students and their families by tapping into sources inside the school system.

25. **D**

ADD is not affiliated with low IQ scores.

26. **D**

A teacher's close proximity establishes a climate that encourages students' active engagement.

27. **C**

Rules help to teach a student what is expected and encourage personal responsibility.

28. **B**

The teacher is facilitating conflict resolution in a negative manner—which doesn't work.

29. **D**

Effective praise works best when it is used in conjunction with a particular achievement.

30. **A**

When students evaluate their own performance, they effectively learn to self-reinforce and grow to need less praise from others.

31. **B**

Expectations should challenge the students and motivate them to accomplish more.

32. **C**

The teacher provides instruction and models all necessary parts of the activity to assure complete understanding.

33. **D**

It is necessary to emphasize major concepts and big ideas rather than basic skills with at-risk students to allow them to see the "big picture."

34. **A**

The knowledge of government and society is not necessarily a professional knowledge base for teachers.

35. **C**

Physical attributes and demand for absolute obedience do not make for an effective teacher.

36. **C**

Reflection helps teachers to look at unique situations in depth.

37. **A**

Research has always shown the influence that teachers have on a student's achievement.

38. **D**

Managing an instructional environment through rules, respect, and good preparation prevents discipline problems.

39. **A**

A teacher's close proximity establishes a climate that requires students' active attention.

40. **C**

When students are overtired, they cannot perform to their potential.

41. **B**

The definition for a mastery orientation to motivation is that effort is linked to learning and that learning is inherently satisfying.

42. **D**

Social skills is the fourth characteristic of cooperative learning, not individual work.

43. **C**

Self-regulated learning is when the student puts forth his/her best effort.

44. **A**

Teachers must adjust communication to promote student understanding and engagement.

45. **A**

Teachers must make changes to their strategies for communication to reach all students.

46. **C**

A true-false test is not a form of cooperative groups and pairs.

47. **B**

Students need teachers to direct them on how to monitor their behavior.

48. **C**

Writing the formula for the area of a rectangle on a test is not a method to determine an authentic assessment.

49. **D**

It is the teacher's method in teaching that needs to adapt to the cultural and behavioral diversity in the classroom.

50. **D**

Nearly 12% of students are enrolled in special education programs.

51. **B**

Dyspepsia is NOT a disorder that disrupts the student's learning process.

52. **C**

With the right support and intervention, these students can adapt to their disabilities and thrive in school.

53. **B**

Effective classroom routines help students to cope with distractions and changes in the classroom.

54. **C**

A classroom management plan is student-to-teacher oriented and not parent oriented.

55. **A**

Poverty is one of the many possibilities for the high number of dropouts.

56. **D**

We must adapt our teaching methods to meet the learning needs of all students.

57. **A**

Students at vastly different levels will have different needs. These will need to be recognized and addressed.

58. **C**

Ms. Logan needs to focus on brevity and clarity in creating her classroom procedures.

59. **B**

A teacher has to plan for differences among students and will need to create assignments accordingly.

60. **D**

Successful classroom management is centered on positive-reinforcement.

Sample Responses for Constructed-Response Questions

Writing Samples with a Score of 3

1. As a seventh grade math teacher the pressure to teach content, content, content is intense. In the grand scheme of things, content instruction, whether in math, science, language arts or social studies, is in a complete and continuing state of flux. New knowledge is added to the disciplines on a daily basis. Math "facts" change as we look at new discoveries in quantum physics, our understanding of science alters with each new look at the universe using both nano technology and space exploration; language arts changes almost hourly as new words and different cultures interact with our own; even the staid "facts" of history are continually updated. Teaching students the "facts" of our content therefore, is an exercise in futility.

How then do we prepare our students for a world that is in their future? Developing critical thinking in our students—the ability to climb Bloom's Taxonomy—is arguably a far more important task to accomplish. Andy Warhol noted that "the medium is the message." We need to use the medium of our discipline (mathematics) to deliver the message of critical thinking skills to our students.

Costa's concepts, termed "Habits of the Mind," help us to use our medium to deliver this important message. Issues such as; perseverance, flexibility, humor, and accuracy, focused on in our classroom management and teaching strategies serve to nudge students away from pure content to address the questions of concept, synthesis, analysis, and problem solving.

The way in which we ask questions, assess our students, prepare instruction, and use technology, all direct our students to understand the nature of our discipline, rather than the content of our subject. In mathematics it is far more effective for our students to have learned a variety of strategies that they can use to solve a problem, than to have memorized a series of formulas.

2.   It is important that I establish ground rules early in the semester. I would let my students know that disruptive behavior will not be tolerated in the classroom. That way, my students will feel more comfortable knowing where the boundaries are. The following are some methods I can use to handle or deter disruptive behavior:

Depending on the infraction, the best response might be simply to ignore certain antagonistic behavior. If, however, the student persists in exhibiting blatantly aggressive or other hostile behaviors, it may be necessary to take more drastic action. I might have to ask the student to leave the classroom, or, depending on the infraction, use the behavior as a springboard into a class discussion on social etiquette.

Also, other students might intervene instead of waiting for my reaction or response. They might exert the necessary peer pressure to squelch the situation before it escalates. Some might say that this is my responsibility, not that of the students. However, the classroom is an environment for learning on a holistic level, so that I need to take advantage of any pedagogical opportunity.

Regardless, I must curb disruptive infractions early so that I will remain the person in charge. This can prevent further situations from getting out of hand.

Evaluation of Sample Responses

1. Purpose:
The writer addressed the topic from the standpoint of her future seventh grade class giving clear examples of needed student focus on learning rather than on mere content.

Application of Content Knowledge and Skills:
The writing sample gives evidence of a well-rounded knowledge of classroom management and teaching strategies.

Supporting Evidence:
More than adequate supporting evidence is cited.

2. Purpose:

The passage has a clearly formulated, precise, specific, and focused thesis. The author defines the central terms well and accurately employs them. The author demonstrates a clear sense of purpose.

Application of Content Knowledge and Skills:

This essay does a good job of answering the question. It can be difficult to know how to answer generalized questions where the apparent answer, as this question acknowledges, "depends on the individual situation." In other words, the writer responds to the question to the best of her ability. The essay conveys the impression that the writer is thinking seriously about the question and its objective. The essay answered the question asked by exemplifying various responses toward disruptive behavior in the classroom. For that reason, it addresses the assignment well.

Supporting Evidence:

Adding to the essay's sophistication level is the fact that it flows logically and attempts persuasively to address an opposing viewpoint and/or alternative idea.

Practice Test 2

GACE Professional Pedagogy
(Code 172)

1. Ⓐ Ⓑ Ⓒ Ⓓ   16. Ⓐ Ⓑ Ⓒ Ⓓ   31. Ⓐ Ⓑ Ⓒ Ⓓ   46. Ⓐ Ⓑ Ⓒ Ⓓ

2. Ⓐ Ⓑ Ⓒ Ⓓ   17. Ⓐ Ⓑ Ⓒ Ⓓ   32. Ⓐ Ⓑ Ⓒ Ⓓ   47. Ⓐ Ⓑ Ⓒ Ⓓ

3. Ⓐ Ⓑ Ⓒ Ⓓ   18. Ⓐ Ⓑ Ⓒ Ⓓ   33. Ⓐ Ⓑ Ⓒ Ⓓ   48. Ⓐ Ⓑ Ⓒ Ⓓ

4. Ⓐ Ⓑ Ⓒ Ⓓ   19. Ⓐ Ⓑ Ⓒ Ⓓ   34. Ⓐ Ⓑ Ⓒ Ⓓ   49. Ⓐ Ⓑ Ⓒ Ⓓ

5. Ⓐ Ⓑ Ⓒ Ⓓ   20. Ⓐ Ⓑ Ⓒ Ⓓ   35. Ⓐ Ⓑ Ⓒ Ⓓ   50. Ⓐ Ⓑ Ⓒ Ⓓ

6. Ⓐ Ⓑ Ⓒ Ⓓ   21. Ⓐ Ⓑ Ⓒ Ⓓ   36. Ⓐ Ⓑ Ⓒ Ⓓ   51. Ⓐ Ⓑ Ⓒ Ⓓ

7. Ⓐ Ⓑ Ⓒ Ⓓ   22. Ⓐ Ⓑ Ⓒ Ⓓ   37. Ⓐ Ⓑ Ⓒ Ⓓ   52. Ⓐ Ⓑ Ⓒ Ⓓ

8. Ⓐ Ⓑ Ⓒ Ⓓ   23. Ⓐ Ⓑ Ⓒ Ⓓ   38. Ⓐ Ⓑ Ⓒ Ⓓ   53. Ⓐ Ⓑ Ⓒ Ⓓ

9. Ⓐ Ⓑ Ⓒ Ⓓ   24. Ⓐ Ⓑ Ⓒ Ⓓ   39. Ⓐ Ⓑ Ⓒ Ⓓ   54. Ⓐ Ⓑ Ⓒ Ⓓ

10. Ⓐ Ⓑ Ⓒ Ⓓ   25. Ⓐ Ⓑ Ⓒ Ⓓ   40. Ⓐ Ⓑ Ⓒ Ⓓ   55. Ⓐ Ⓑ Ⓒ Ⓓ

11. Ⓐ Ⓑ Ⓒ Ⓓ   26. Ⓐ Ⓑ Ⓒ Ⓓ   41. Ⓐ Ⓑ Ⓒ Ⓓ   56. Ⓐ Ⓑ Ⓒ Ⓓ

12. Ⓐ Ⓑ Ⓒ Ⓓ   27. Ⓐ Ⓑ Ⓒ Ⓓ   42. Ⓐ Ⓑ Ⓒ Ⓓ   57. Ⓐ Ⓑ Ⓒ Ⓓ

13. Ⓐ Ⓑ Ⓒ Ⓓ   28. Ⓐ Ⓑ Ⓒ Ⓓ   43. Ⓐ Ⓑ Ⓒ Ⓓ   58. Ⓐ Ⓑ Ⓒ Ⓓ

14. Ⓐ Ⓑ Ⓒ Ⓓ   29. Ⓐ Ⓑ Ⓒ Ⓓ   44. Ⓐ Ⓑ Ⓒ Ⓓ   59. Ⓐ Ⓑ Ⓒ Ⓓ

15. Ⓐ Ⓑ Ⓒ Ⓓ   30. Ⓐ Ⓑ Ⓒ Ⓓ   45. Ⓐ Ⓑ Ⓒ Ⓓ   60. Ⓐ Ⓑ Ⓒ Ⓓ

Practice Test 2 (Code 172)

Directions: Circle the best answer then mark it on your answer sheet.

1. Student feedback is an important part of the student/teacher equation. As a new teacher, which of the following is the best way to nurture that equation?

    A. Always grade everything students hand in with a numerical grade.

    B. Use clear "alpha" grades on all student work. Students all understand the alpha system.

    C. Use rubrics for expectations and assignment of grades on students' work.

    D. Grades aren't feedback; use a written narrative only.

2. The primary role of student evaluation is to

    A. rank the order of students in terms of achievement.

    B. have students eventually able to evaluate their own work.

    C. allow parents to know how their child is doing in school.

    D. give teachers a means of punishing/rewarding students.

3. The first step in student instruction is

    A. knowing what students should know and be able to do.

    B. coming up with a creative lesson.

    C. determining what the standardized test expects students to know.

    D. remembering what you really enjoyed learning at their age.

4. Essential elements of cooperative learning include

    A. purposeful grouping.

    B. neutral interdependence.

    C. advance organizers.

    D. summative assessment.

5. The way teachers and students are grouped for instruction and the way time is scheduled in the classroom is known as

   A. classroom organization.

   B. between class ability grouping.

   C. within class ability grouping.

   D. stages of group development.

6. Centralized models of decision-making

   A. recognize different goals for different schools.

   B. cost more than school-based models of decision making.

   C. allow increased parent involvement in the process.

   D. emphasize the importance of standardization among schools.

7. The No Child Left Behind Act

   A. increases funding for all schools.

   B. holds school districts accountable for their performance.

   C. does not allow school choice.

   D. establishes Charter Schools.

8. Inclusion is an increasingly common tactic used to address the needs of all learners. To make this strategy work for classroom teachers, they need to be taught

   A. about Special Education techniques.

   B. to do homogeneous in-class grouping.

   C. to do heterogeneous in-class grouping.

   D. differentiated learning techniques.

9. Most teachers use textbooks in their classes. The advantage of this is

   A. teachers don't have to create their own lessons. They can use those that come with the textbook.

   B. textbooks make public and accessible the private world of the classroom.

   C. the teacher is no longer accountable for the veracity of the content.

   D. there are questions at the end of every chapter that can be assigned for homework.

10. All of the following are components of a lesson plan EXCEPT

    A. the unit description.

    B. learning targets/goals/standards.

    C. a disciplinary code.

    E. assessment.

11. Teaching involves all of the following EXCEPT

    A. creating lesson plans.

    B. going home early and having the summer off.

    C. developing curriculum.

    D. creating rubrics.

12. In selecting appropriate learning materials for the classroom, a teacher must be very familiar with

    A. the requirements of her principal.

    B. the interests of her students.

    C. state-mandated competencies as expressed in the state standards.

    D. what her students' parents will want her to teach.

13. Teachers use a variety of formal and informal assessment strategies in an effective classroom. The clearest definition of an informal assessment is

    A. an assessment that is data driven and a standardized measure of student performance.

    B. an assessment that is not data driven, but rather content and performance driven.

    C. subjective in nature.

    D. an objective measure of performance.

14. Formal or standardized measures of assessment are used to determine a student's achievement compared to his peer group. A criterion-referenced test (informal assessment)

   A. is used to inform instruction.

   B. measures a student's performance compared to a set criteria.

   C. measures a student's growth academically.

   D. reinforces cross-age ability grouping.

15. Teachers need to set learning goals for their students, so that there is a clear picture of what is required. Theses learning goals help teachers do all of the following EXCEPT

   A. clarify what students are to accomplish.

   B. guide assessment of what students have learned.

   C. select methods materials and assignments that are most effective.

   D. establish norm-referenced ability grouping.

16. Indirect instruction methods are the strategy of choice for teachers when which of the following outcomes are desired?

   A. Attitudes, values, or interpersonal outcomes are desired.

   B. Quick dissemination of information is desired.

   C. Classroom control is an issue.

   D. Covering material in a set period of time is a concern.

17. Experiential instruction was one of the favored strategies taught by Mrs. Dailey's professors of education when she was in college. She uses this strategy frequently with her 4th graders because she finds that

   A. her students are more motivated because they actively participate and teach one another.

   B. it often gets her out of the classroom with her class, and she finds the classroom confining.

   C. it is much easier to prepare her lesson plans this way.

   D. she doesn't have to worry about other teachers complaining about how noisy her class is.

18. A good strategy for beginning a lesson is to

    A. provide a three-minute journal exercise for students using a concept from the previous day's lesson.

    B. jump directly into the new lesson.

    C. do a ten-minute review of the previous day's lesson.

    D. explain to students what behaviors are expected in the day ahead.

19. A good exit strategy for a lesson is to

    A. direct students to write a brief exit ticket to summarize what they learned during that class.

    B. assign homework.

    C. dramatically close the textbook.

    D. wait for students to be completely settled before you dismiss them.

20. Effective instruction includes the following principles EXCEPT

    A. the activation principle.

    B. the application principle.

    C. the achievement principle.

    D. the demonstration principle.

21. Using technology in the classroom is no longer an option. When students use computers in school they receive all of the following benefits EXCEPT

    A. essential 21st century skills.

    B. increased motivation.

    C. immediate feedback.

    D. enhanced social development.

22. The "Leave it to Beaver" family concept of the 1950s is long gone. Mom no longer waits at home with milk and cookies for the children when they get out of school. The actual characteristics of the American 21st century family include all of the following EXCEPT

   A. seventy percent of women with children are in the workforce.

   B. six percent of total households in the U.S. have a father that works and a mother that does not work outside the home.

   C. forty-seven percent of U.S. families are single parent, or blended families.

   D. because of obesity issues parents are discouraged from giving their children milk and cookies.

23. Parent responsibility at the school includes all of the following EXCEPT

   A. monitoring student attendance.

   B. doing student homework.

   C. reading and responding to all school reports concerning student behavioral and academic progress.

   D. monitoring the amount of TV/computer/telephone time that is not related to school functions.

24. The school's responsibilities to the parents do NOT include

   A. access to textbooks.

   B. information about the curriculum.

   C. providing a supper for students who are in need.

   D. providing information on a students behavioral and academic progress.

25. Studies indicate that the results of family involvement in a child's school produces

   A. lower grades for the student.

   B. high student achievement.

   C. lower expectations for student success.

   D. resentment on the part of faculty.

26. The characteristics of a community school include all of the following EXCEPT

    A. parents are full partners in their child's education.

    B. parents expect high standards and increased accountability.

    C. parents are expected to teach some of the classes.

    D. the community contributes to a safe and secure school environment.

27. All of the following are forms of diversity experienced in American classrooms in the 21st century EXCEPT

    A. language.

    B. culture.

    C. ability differences.

    D. authority.

28. The issues in American schools have evolved over the years. In the 1950s the primary concerns in public schools were issues such as tardiness, gum chewing, and violations of the dress code. Today's issues are more concerned with the following, EXCEPT

    A. harassment.

    B. homelessness.

    C. teenage pregnancy.

    D. segregation.

29. School dress codes have to meet certain requirements of the law to be enforceable. This is a result of the 1969 Supreme Court case *Tinker v. Des Moines*. What specific issues do dress codes need to concern to be legal?

    A. Modesty and decency

    B. Safety and security

    C. Cleanliness and godliness

    D. Community standards

30. Teachers' rights include all of the following EXCEPT

    A. tenure.

    B. academic freedom.

    C. nondiscrimination.

    D. occupational security.

31. Since teachers act *in loco parentis*, they have all of the following responsibilities and rights towards students assigned to them EXCEPT

   A. supervision.

   B. physical discipline.

   C. guidance.

   D. education.

32. Teachers are typically granted tenure after three to five years of successful teaching. Tenure provides a teacher with

   A. a job for life.

   B. protection from firing.

   C. due process.

   D. seniority.

33. Teachers' responsibilities include

   A. a duty and standard of care that includes providing a safe environment for students.

   B. a requirement to ensure all students are fed a nutritious lunch.

   C. a right to copy any and all materials needed to instruct their students.

   D. a duty to maintain order in the classroom using whatever means is effective.

34. Joan has forgotten her permission slip for a trip to the zoo with Mrs. Farquar's 4th grade class. Mrs. Farquar should

   A. contact Joan's parent and get permission before she includes her on the trip. If that can't be done, Joan must be left at the school.

   B. take her anyway since Mrs. Farquar is Joan's next door neighbor. She knows Joan's mom wouldn't mind.

   C. ignore the requirement for a permission slip because Joan is very forgetful and probably had one originally.

   D. leave Joan with the principal and take the rest of the class to the zoo.

35. Once you have finished creating the content area of your lesson plan, you must finish the details, which include

    A. collecting resources, deciding on homework assignments and handouts, and making any copies necessary.

    B. creating the assessment.

    C. deciding which standard you have addressed.

    D. determining the teaching strategy you will use.

36. When proctoring standardized tests it is important to be aware of each of the following EXCEPT

    A. distracting noise.

    B. ventilation in the testing room.

    C. parental disapproval.

    D. student fatigue.

37. What is the difference between authentic assessment and performance assessment?

    A. Authentic assessment involves portfolios.

    B. Performance assessment involves summative evaluation.

    C. Authentic assessment involves formative assessment.

    D. There is no difference; both refer to direct measures of student outcomes.

38. When teachers measure students' attainment of knowledge and skills for the purpose of making decisions about their teaching, they are engaged in

    A. measurement.

    B. alternative assessment.

    C. formative evaluation.

    D. summative evaluation.

39. Innovations in assessment are partly a response to criticisms of the fairness and objectivity of standardized tests that have focused on all of the following EXCEPT

    A. class and gender bias.

    B. failure to measure student's general level of intelligence.

    C. failure to accurately measure student's skills.

    D. failure to measure students' levels of achievement.

40.   Which of the following is NOT an example of authentic assessment?

   A.   Writing a travel brochure about your town

   B.   Making a map of your town

   C.   Writing the formula for the area of a rectangle on a test

   D.   Producing a video about your town

41.   A curriculum guide states: "Students will demonstrate mastery of addition and subtraction." This is an example of

   A.   official curriculum.

   B.   operational curriculum.

   C.   extracurricula.

   D.   null curriculum.

42.   Which of the following has been a criticism leveled at American textbooks?

   A.   Their writing style is fragmented and choppy.

   B.   They suffer from curriculum overload, cramming too much information into individual books.

   C.   There are too many irrelevant illustrations.

   D.   All of the above.

43.   How are standardized tests useful in assessment?

   A.   For teacher evaluation

   B.   For evaluation of the administration

   C.   For comparison from school to school

   D.   For comparison to the population to which the test was normed

44.   An alternative assessment is a(n)

   A.   traditional large-scale assessment.

   B.   individualized diagnostic assessment.

   C.   assessment device common to all learners.

   D.   assessment of a unique array of goals and experiences.

45.   A test is said to be valid when it

    A.   is fair and free from teacher bias.

    B.   measures what it claims to measure.

    C.   produces consistent results over time.

    D.   has safeguards against cultural bias.

46.   A test is said to be reliable when it

    A.   is fair and free from teacher bias.

    B.   measures what it claims to measure.

    C.   produces consistent results over time.

    D.   has safeguards against cultural bias.

47.   Which of the following is an advantage of objective test items?

    A.   They are fairer to students.

    B.   They allow greater coverage of topics.

    C.   They eliminate guessing.

    D.   They are easier to mark than other test items.

48.   Students in Mr. Davis's fifth-grade class are asked to collect various artifacts of their work and put the work in a notebook to demonstrate what they can do for their parents and teacher. This is an example of

    A.   essay assessment.

    B.   authentic assessment.

    C.   portfolio assessment.

    D.   performance assessment.

49.   Teachers need to continue to grow throughout their careers; otherwise they risk becoming the fossils they made fun of when they were in school. All of the following methods can be used to self-monitor teacher growth EXCEPT

    A.   reviewing lesson plans for currency and relevance.

    B.   brainstorming other approaches to content with peers.

    C.   identifying the lessons that worked, and keeping them in a file to re-use over and over again.

    D.   attending teacher workshops and conventions.

50. Barry is one of your students; his parents are deaf. Barry is failing science and you want to contact the parents. How should you proceed?

    A. Do all communication in writing.

    B. You obviously can't communicate with them since you don't sign, so deal with Barry only.

    C. Turn the issues over to the guidance office since you aren't prepared to deal with it.

    D. Talk to your administrator about finding an appropriate interpreter to help you communicate with the parents personally.

51. Which of the following should NOT be a purpose of a parent-teacher conference?

    A. To involve the parent in their child's education

    B. To establish a friendship with the child's parents

    C. To resolve a concern about the child's performance

    D. To inform parents about positive behaviors of the child

52. When communicating with parents who are ESOL (English for Speakers of Other Languages), you should

    A. provide materials whenever possible in their native language.

    B. provide the same communication that you would to native English speaking parents.

    C. expect all parents to find their own way of interpreting your messages.

    D. expect that they communicate in English because that is the language in which all classes are taught in the school.

53. Although Georgia is a right-to-work state, teacher unions are still involved in public education. The unions do all of the following EXCEPT

    A. provide professional development.

    B. advocate for teachers' rights.

    C. be involved in collective bargaining for teachers' salaries.

    D. develop professional codes and practices.

54. When decision-making is set to a centralized model in a school district it

    A. causes school expenses to rise.

    B. encourages individual schools to set their own goals.

    C. draws more parent support.

    D. increases the standardization of goals and procedures throughout the district.

55. Which of the following could be used to improve teaching skills?

    A. Developing a professional development plan

    B. Using self-evaluation and reflection

    C. Building professional learning communities

    D. All of the above

56. Teachers' responsibilities include all of the following EXCEPT

    A. the practice of ethical behavior.

    B. the ability to pass the reasonable and prudent test.

    C. to report suspected child abuse to the parent involved.

    D. to avoid sexual harassment in word and deed.

57. The Individuals with Disabilities Education Act defines students with special needs as all of the following EXCEPT

    A. those with mental retardation.

    B. those who are gifted and talented.

    C. those with speech or language impairments.

    D. those with an emotional disturbance.

58. IDEA has basic principles that address how educational services will be provided to identified students. They include all of the following EXCEPT

    A. services must be provided by specially trained teachers in a private environment.

    B. education must be offered in the least restrictive environment.

    C. services must adequately address the student's needs.

    D. age, past achievement, and parental expectations must be considered.

59. Who may refer students to the Special Education process?

   A. A medical doctor

   B. A parent

   C. A school official

   D. All of the above

60. Under the Georgia Code of Ethics for Teachers, disciplinary action may be taken by the PSC for all of the following EXCEPT

   A. the abuse of students.

   B. joining a teachers' union.

   C. failure to make a required report.

   D. the abandonment of a contract.

Directions: Constructed-Response questions are short essay questions that ask you to respond to a question indicating the grade level you are prepared to teach. Your response is scored on purpose, application of content knowledge and skill, and supporting evidence. It is not a test of your writing ability. Clarity is important. Be articulate and succinct, write legibly, in English, and focus on the topic of the question.

Constructed-Response Questions (Test Code 172)

1. *Address the following with the subject area and grade level you are prepared to teach.*

   - *Explain what instructional strategies you would use for a diverse class of students.*

   - *Explain what diversities you would expect these strategies to address.*

   - *Explain why the strategies you have chosen would be effective.*

2. *You realize that most of the students in your class do not use the library, watch TV in English, or read in English at home.*

- *Identify your grade level and subject.*

- *Describe two strategies that you could use to encourage reading in the home;*

- *Explain how you might get your students to use the local library that is within a block of the school;*

- *Identify two resources you could access to help make sure that your students have access to educational materials.*

Practice Test 2 (Code 172) Answer Key

Question	Answer	Competency
1.	C	7
2.	B	7
3.	A	8
4.	A	8
5.	A	8
6.	D	10
7.	B	7
8.	D	9
9.	B	9
10.	C	9
11.	B	9
12.	C	9
13.	B	7
14.	A	7
15.	D	8
16.	B	8
17.	A	8
18.	A	9
19.	A	9
20.	C	9
21.	D	9
22.	D	9
23.	B	10
24.	C	10
25.	B	10
26.	C	10
27.	D	10
28.	D	10
29.	B	10
30.	D	11

31.	B	11
32.	C	11
33.	A	11
34.	A	11
35.	A	8
36.	C	7
37.	D	7
38.	C	7
39.	B	7
40.	C	7
41.	A	8
42.	D	7
43.	D	7
44.	D	7
45.	B	7
46.	C	7
47.	B	7
48.	C	7
49.	C	11
50.	D	10
51.	B	10
52.	A	10
53.	C	11
54.	D	11
55.	D	10
56.	B	12
57.	B	12
58.	A	12
59.	D	12
60.	B	12

Practice Test 2 (Code 172) Progress Chart

Competency 7

1	2	7	13	14	36	37	38	39	40	44	43	44	45	46	47	48

___/17

Competency 8

3	4	5	15	16	17	35	41

___/8

Competency 9

8	9	10	11	12	18	19	20	21	22

___/10

Competency 10

6	23	24	25	26	27	28	29	50	51	52	55

___/12

Competency 11

30	31	32	33	34	49	53	54

___/8

Competency 12

56	57	58	59	60

___/5

Detailed Explanations for Practice Test 2 (Code 172)

1. **C**

   Rubrics serve both student and teacher best when they are used as a tool to give reference points for expectations of student work and achievement.

2. **B**

   Student evaluation allows for self-evaluation and self-correction as the students proceed through their work.

3. **A**

   Teachers should be able to demonstrate knowledge of key factors to consider in planning instruction.

4. **A**

   Grouping done with a clear purpose is one of the essential elements of cooperative learning.

5. **A**

   This is often called organizing for instruction.

6. **D**

   Centralized decision making is the process in which decisions are made for the whole by a single source.

7. **B**

   NCLB is based on the belief that setting high standards and establishing measurable goals to which districts are held can improve educational outcomes.

8. **D**

   Because of the diversity of the student population in the classrooms, traditional teaching practices are being replaced with differentiated learning techniques.

9. **B**

   Textbooks are the most efficient way to make public and accessible the private world of the classroom.

10. **C**

    Besides the items listed, lesson plans must also consider students' development, characteristics and prior experiences; students' current knowledge and skills; available time and resources; and the type of content or skills to be taught.

11. **B**

Even though we may want to think that teaching ends at the ring of the bell, that isn't realistic.

12. **C**

Teachers must use the Georgia Performance Standards to guide the lesson.

13. **B**

An informal assessment is best defined as an assessment that *is not* data driven, but rather content and performance driven.

14. **A**

This form of testing is used as an interpretive frame of reference for a specified content domain, rather than a specified population of persons.

15. **D**

Note also that the communication of expectations to students more effectively is a learning goal that is not mentioned here.

16. **B**

Also, note that indirect instruction strategies are student-centered.

17. **A**

Also, note that experiential instruction strategies are student-centered. The emphasis is on process, not product.

18. **A**

In this way you can relate your new lesson to situations or knowledge that your learners are already familiar with, e.g., the previous lesson.

19. **A**

At a different time you can use a quiz or assignment to confirm mastery of your objectives.

20. **C**

The activation, demonstration, and application principle are three principles of effective instruction.

21. **D**

Effective technology integration must happen across the curriculum in ways that show a deep and enhanced learning process.

22. **D**

While obesity is an issue among our youth population, excessive milk and cookies has nothing to do with it.

23. **B**

Students need to do their own homework.

24. **C**

Besides the three listed, the school is also responsible for distributing accurate and timely information to parents about school functions and activities to the parents.

25. **B**

Research from the Department of Education indicates that the students benefit from the communication between the home and the school.

26. **C**

While parents are full partners in their child's education, they are not expected to teach classes.

27. **D**

Note that students with exceptionalities are another form of diversity within the classroom.

28. **D**

Segregation was banned in the mid-twentieth century.

29. **B**

Above all else, the safety and security of students is most important in the learning environment.

30. **D**

Occupational security is not listed as a teacher's right.

31. **B**

Teachers are responsible for supervising, guiding, and educating students. They may not use physical discipline.

32. **C**

Tenure provides a teacher with "due process."

33. **A**

Teachers are responsible for providing a standard of care that includes a safe environment for students.

34. **A**

It is the school's responsibility to distribute accurate and timely information to parents about school functions and activities, along with following safety guidelines set by the school board.

35. **A**

Teachers must ask themselves, "Does this lesson plan use appropriate tools, resources, and information conflicts by validating information through research and comparison of data?"

36. **C**

Teachers are responsible for the room conditions in which standardized tests are administered.

37. **D**

Performance-based assessments ask students to show what they can do given an authentic *task* which is then judged using a specific set of criteria.

38. **C**

Formative evaluation is the process in which teachers measure students' attainment of knowledge and skills for the purpose of making decisions about their teaching.

39. **B**

It is believed that a wide variety of assessment tools should be incorporated in order to evaluate all aspects of the education students receive.

40. **C**

Writing the formula for the area of a rectangle on a test is not an example of authentic assessment.

41. **A**

Teachers in the State of Georgia plan their lessons according to the Georgia Performance Standards.

42. **D**

American textbooks have been criticized as having too many irrelevant illustrations, too much curriculum, and a writing style that is often fragmented and choppy.

43. **D**

Standardized assessments may be norm-referenced or criterion-referenced.

44. **D**

Alternative assessment also serves as a tool to assess a broad spectrum of learners.

45. **B**

If a test is valid, it is almost always reliable.

46. **C**

Reliability refers to the measure in which assessments are consistent and also reflect on the consistency of assessment scores.

47. **B**

Objective tests allow the testing over a greater coverage of topics.

48. **C**

A portfolio assessment can be an examination of student-selected samples of work experiences and documents related to outcomes being assessed.

49. **C**

The activity and practice of becoming a lifelong learner is of importance to continued growth as a professional educator.

50. **D**

It is the responsibility of the school to meet the needs of students through catering to the particular family arrangement in which the student lives.

51. **B**

The parent-teacher conference is a method of communicating with parents about their children's success or failure in school.

52. **A**

More commonly these days, teachers are meeting with and discussing the student's academic life with a language minority parent or family.

53. **C**

Although they don't have collective-bargaining rights as unions do in other states, they do provide significant professional development activities as do other professional organizations.

54. **D**

Centralized models of decision making emphasizes the importance of standardization among schools.

55. **D**

Developing a professional development plan by using self-evaluation and reflection and building professional learning communities are all methods to improve teaching skills.

56. **B**

A teacher's responsibilities also include providing a standard of care that includes providing a safe environment, providing proper instruction, and supervising students.

57. **B**

Students with mental retardation, speech or language impairments, and/or with an emotional disturbance are all protected under the Individuals with Disabilities Education Act.

58. **A**

In 1975 the Individuals with Disabilities Education Act was passed, providing for the education of all children in the least restrictive environment.

59. **D**

Students are referred to this process by a parent, teacher, school official or a doctor/other professional.

60. **B**

Teachers may, and often do, join unions (e.g., NEA, AFT). The unions in Georgia are not "closed shop," however, since Georgia is a "right-to-work" state.

Sample Responses for Constructed-Response Questions

Writing Samples with a Score of 3

1. My fourth grade class is preparing for the state standardized test (such as the CRCT). The class is from an urban district with little or no racial or ethnic diversity; however, this class is an inclusion class and has a high level of diversity in ability and skills. In order to best serve all of these students a variety of teaching strategies need to be used. The term used for dealing with this type

of diversity is differentiated instruction. This strategy involves establishing a standards-based goal for the entire class, while providing individual paths to reach the goal. This allows students with different learning styles, and different levels of prior knowledge to still attain the instructional standard within a given range of time. Although this method is based on individual needs, students can often be placed into clusters or groups to decrease the amount of preparation time, and to more efficiently use classroom instructional time.

In order to bring my class to the level of standards required by the CRCT, instruction will be developed around the state standards addressed by this test. An evaluation of the performance level of each student, and their preferred learning style will be established. Instructional strategies will then be developed around clusters of students with similar profiles. The differentiation needs to be augmented with whole group instruction, cooperative learning, cross age tutoring, and peer tutoring, in order to have a well rounded and egalitarian approach.

2. I will be teaching a multi-ethnic third grade class in the fall. This specific need could be an important opportunity to make new friends, find help for my students, and involve the adults in improving their own language skills. The first thing I would do— since I am not bilingual—is to find someone who will help interpret for me during parent conferences and classroom visitation sessions.

I will give parents some important information, that being: the best way for them to help the children learn to read is to read to them and with them. Because some parents cannot read themselves, I will provide this information orally with the help of the interpreter. I can provide a list of books for the children to take with them to the library. If their parents are not able to find the books, this list will be a resource when they or the children ask for help. If the adults are non-readers, I might suggest that the responsible adult just provide a time for the child to practice reading and actually sit and listen to the child read.

If the interpreter and I can make sure that the parents understand the importance of regular family visits to the library, we will have achieved a major goal. I might even ask a librarian to come to the school and help the parents to sign up for a library card for themselves and their children. Perhaps I can get the local library to host an event for children that might not be too stressful for those families that have never used a library.

I might collect also magazines that the children can check out and take home for the entire family to read. I could also send home a list of some educational television programs that the families can watch together.

Evaluation of Sample Responses

1. Purpose:

The writer answers the question in the specific arena of a standardized testing situation with a clear explanation of the class population.

Application of Content Knowledge and Skills:

The application of learned strategies for the given situation is well done.

Supporting Evidence:

The writer gives clear examples of methods to be used for the situation. These methods include whole group instruction, cooperative learning and peer tutoring.

2. Purpose:

The essay is an excellent example of a good answer. The essay answers each question asked in a simple, straightforward way.

Application of Content Knowledge and Skills:

The solutions are feasible and reasonable. The writer provides specific examples for each part of the question.

Supporting Evidence:

The writer shows understanding of the principles of learning and teaching. The essay flows logically and is well organized. It is a model answer.

Index